50 Quick and Easy Weeknight Recipes for Home

By: Kelly Johnson

Table of Contents

- Spaghetti Carbonara
- Stir-fried Chicken and Vegetables
- Beef Tacos
- Lemon Garlic Shrimp Pasta
- Chicken Stir-fry with Cashews
- One-Pot Chili Mac
- Baked Parmesan Chicken
- Teriyaki Salmon
- Creamy Tomato Basil Soup
- Veggie Fried Rice
- BBQ Pulled Pork Sandwiches
- Beef and Broccoli Stir-fry
- Margherita Pizza
- Garlic Butter Shrimp Scampi
- Thai Red Curry
- Pesto Pasta with Cherry Tomatoes
- Turkey Burgers
- Mushroom Risotto
- Honey Garlic Chicken Thighs
- Veggie Quesadillas
- Lemon Herb Grilled Chicken
- Sausage and Peppers
- Caprese Salad
- Pan-seared Scallops
- Cajun Jambalaya
- Mediterranean Couscous Salad
- Orange Glazed Pork Chops
- Ratatouille
- Beef and Bean Burritos
- Garlic Butter Steak Bites
- Chicken Caesar Salad Wraps
- Tomato Basil Bruschetta
- Pad Thai
- Italian Sausage Pasta
- Lemon Herb Roasted Vegetables

- Hawaiian BBQ Chicken Pizza
- Pork Stir-fry with Snow Peas
- Quinoa Stuffed Bell Peppers
- Chicken Enchiladas
- Creamy Mushroom Soup
- Shrimp Fried Rice
- Greek Lemon Chicken Skewers
- Sweet and Sour Meatballs
- Caprese Pasta Salad
- Butternut Squash Risotto
- BBQ Chicken Quesadillas
- Garlic Parmesan Roasted Shrimp
- Turkey Meatloaf
- Veggie Stir-fry with Tofu
- Lemon Garlic Butter Salmon

Spaghetti Carbonara

Ingredients:

- 350g spaghetti
- 150g guanciale or pancetta, diced (you can also use bacon if necessary)
- 3 large eggs
- 50g Pecorino Romano cheese, grated (you can also use Parmesan)
- Freshly ground black pepper
- Salt (for pasta water)

Instructions:

1. Prepare the pasta:
   - Bring a large pot of salted water to a boil. Cook the spaghetti according to the package instructions until al dente.
2. Prepare the sauce:
   - While the pasta is cooking, heat a large skillet over medium heat. Add the diced guanciale or pancetta and cook until crispy and golden brown, about 5-7 minutes. Remove from heat and set aside.
3. Prepare the egg mixture:
   - In a bowl, whisk together the eggs, grated Pecorino Romano cheese, and a generous amount of freshly ground black pepper. Mix well until combined.
4. Combine everything:
   - Once the pasta is cooked al dente, reserve about 1 cup of pasta water, then drain the pasta and add it immediately to the skillet with the crispy guanciale or pancetta. Toss well to combine.
5. Add the egg mixture:
   - Immediately pour the egg and cheese mixture over the hot pasta. Toss quickly and vigorously to coat the pasta evenly. The heat from the pasta will cook the eggs and create a creamy sauce. If needed, add a splash of the reserved pasta water to loosen the sauce.
6. Serve:
   - Serve the Spaghetti Carbonara immediately, garnished with additional grated Pecorino Romano cheese and a sprinkle of black pepper on top.

Tips:

- Timing is key: It's important to toss the hot pasta with the egg mixture quickly and off the heat to prevent the eggs from scrambling.
- Creaminess: The dish should be creamy and silky, not dry. Adjust the consistency with reserved pasta water as needed.
- Variations: Some variations include adding garlic or onions, but traditional Carbonara is quite simple with just a few key ingredients.

Enjoy your homemade Spaghetti Carbonara!

Stir-fried Chicken and Vegetables

Ingredients:

- 2 boneless, skinless chicken breasts, thinly sliced
- 2 cups mixed vegetables (such as bell peppers, broccoli, snap peas, carrots, mushrooms)
- 2 cloves garlic, minced
- 1-inch piece of ginger, minced or grated
- 2 tablespoons soy sauce
- 1 tablespoon oyster sauce (optional)
- 1 tablespoon hoisin sauce (optional)
- 1 tablespoon cornstarch mixed with 2 tablespoons water (optional, for thickening)
- 2 tablespoons cooking oil (vegetable, peanut, or sesame oil)
- Salt and pepper, to taste
- Cooked rice or noodles, for serving

Instructions:

1. Prepare the chicken:
   - Slice the chicken breasts thinly against the grain. Season with salt and pepper.
2. Prepare the vegetables:
   - Wash and chop the mixed vegetables into bite-sized pieces.
3. Heat the wok or skillet:
   - Heat 1 tablespoon of oil in a large wok or skillet over medium-high heat.
4. Stir-fry the chicken:
   - Add the sliced chicken to the hot pan in a single layer. Let it sear for 1-2 minutes without stirring to get a nice brown color. Then, stir-fry for another 2-3 minutes until the chicken is cooked through and no longer pink. Remove the chicken from the pan and set aside.
5. Cook the vegetables:
   - Add another tablespoon of oil to the pan if needed. Add minced garlic and ginger, stir-frying for about 30 seconds until fragrant.
   - Add the chopped vegetables to the pan. Stir-fry for 3-4 minutes until they are tender-crisp. You can cover the pan for the last minute to steam the vegetables slightly if desired.
6. Combine everything:
   - Return the cooked chicken to the pan with the vegetables. Add soy sauce, oyster sauce, and hoisin sauce (if using). Toss everything together to combine evenly.
7. Thicken the sauce (optional):
   - If you prefer a thicker sauce, push the chicken and vegetables to the sides of the pan. Pour the cornstarch mixture into the center of the pan and stir until it thickens and becomes glossy, about 1 minute.
8. Serve:

- Serve the stir-fried chicken and vegetables hot over cooked rice or noodles.

Tips:

- Preparation is key: Have all your ingredients chopped and ready to go before you start cooking, as stir-frying is a fast process.
- High heat: Ensure your pan is hot enough to sear the chicken and vegetables quickly, maintaining their crispness and preventing them from stewing.
- Customize: Feel free to adjust the vegetables and sauces to your liking. Add more soy sauce or spice it up with a dash of chili sauce if desired.

Enjoy your homemade stir-fried chicken and vegetables! It's a healthy and satisfying meal that can be easily adapted with different ingredients and flavors.

Beef Tacos

Ingredients:

- 1 lb ground beef (preferably lean)
- 1 small onion, finely chopped
- 2 cloves garlic, minced
- 1 tablespoon chili powder
- 1 teaspoon ground cumin
- 1/2 teaspoon paprika
- 1/4 teaspoon cayenne pepper (optional, for heat)
- Salt and pepper, to taste
- 1/2 cup tomato sauce
- 1/4 cup water
- 8-10 small tortillas (corn or flour)
- Toppings: shredded lettuce, diced tomatoes, shredded cheese, sour cream, salsa, guacamole, etc.

Instructions:

1. Cook the beef mixture:
    - In a large skillet or frying pan, heat a bit of oil over medium-high heat. Add the chopped onion and cook until softened, about 3-4 minutes.
    - Add the minced garlic and cook for another 30 seconds until fragrant.
    - Add the ground beef to the skillet, breaking it up with a spatula or spoon. Cook until the beef is browned and cooked through, about 5-6 minutes.
2. Season the beef:
    - Stir in the chili powder, ground cumin, paprika, cayenne pepper (if using), salt, and pepper. Cook for another minute to toast the spices.
3. Add tomato sauce and simmer:
    - Pour in the tomato sauce and water. Stir well to combine. Bring the mixture to a simmer, then reduce the heat to low. Let it simmer gently for 10-15 minutes, stirring occasionally, until the sauce thickens slightly and flavors meld together. If it becomes too dry, add a bit more water.
4. Warm the tortillas:
    - While the beef mixture is simmering, warm the tortillas. You can do this by heating them individually in a dry skillet over medium heat for about 15-20 seconds per side, or by wrapping them in a damp paper towel and microwaving them for 20-30 seconds.
5. Assemble the tacos:
    - Spoon the beef mixture onto each tortilla. Top with your favorite toppings such as shredded lettuce, diced tomatoes, shredded cheese, sour cream, salsa, and guacamole.
6. Serve:

- Serve the beef tacos immediately while warm.

Tips:

- Customize toppings: Feel free to customize your tacos with your favorite toppings. The more variety, the better!
- Tortilla options: Choose between corn or flour tortillas based on your preference. Corn tortillas are traditional for authentic tacos, while flour tortillas offer a softer texture.
- Make it ahead: The beef mixture can be made ahead of time and reheated when ready to serve.

Enjoy your homemade beef tacos! They're perfect for a quick and tasty weeknight meal or for a casual gathering with friends and family.

Lemon Garlic Shrimp Pasta

Ingredients:

- 8 oz (about 225g) spaghetti or linguine pasta
- 1 lb (about 450g) large shrimp, peeled and deveined
- 4 tablespoons unsalted butter, divided
- 4 cloves garlic, minced
- Zest of 1 lemon
- Juice of 1 lemon
- 1/2 cup chicken broth or seafood broth
- Salt and pepper, to taste
- Red pepper flakes (optional, for heat)
- 1/4 cup chopped fresh parsley, for garnish
- Grated Parmesan cheese, for serving

Instructions:

1. Cook the pasta:
   - Cook the spaghetti or linguine pasta according to the package instructions in a large pot of salted boiling water until al dente. Reserve about 1 cup of pasta water, then drain the pasta and set aside.
2. Prepare the shrimp:
   - Pat the shrimp dry with paper towels and season with salt and pepper.
3. Cook the shrimp:
   - In a large skillet, melt 2 tablespoons of butter over medium-high heat. Add the shrimp in a single layer and cook for about 2-3 minutes per side until pink and cooked through. Remove the shrimp from the skillet and set aside.
4. Make the lemon garlic sauce:
   - In the same skillet, melt the remaining 2 tablespoons of butter over medium heat. Add the minced garlic and cook for about 1 minute until fragrant.
5. Add liquids and zest:
   - Stir in the lemon zest, lemon juice, and chicken or seafood broth. Season with salt, pepper, and red pepper flakes (if using). Let the sauce simmer for 2-3 minutes to reduce slightly.
6. Combine everything:
   - Add the cooked pasta to the skillet with the lemon garlic sauce. Toss to coat the pasta evenly with the sauce. If the sauce seems too thick, add some of the reserved pasta water a little at a time until you reach your desired consistency.
7. Add shrimp and garnish:
   - Gently stir in the cooked shrimp to warm through. Taste and adjust seasoning if needed.
   - Remove from heat and sprinkle with chopped fresh parsley.
8. Serve:

- Serve the lemon garlic shrimp pasta immediately, garnished with grated Parmesan cheese if desired.

Tips:

- Fresh ingredients: Using fresh lemon zest and juice really enhances the citrus flavor of the dish.
- Pasta water: The starchy pasta water helps to emulsify the sauce and make it creamy, so don't skip this step.
- Variations: You can add in vegetables like cherry tomatoes, spinach, or asparagus to add more color and nutrition to the dish.

Enjoy your flavorful lemon garlic shrimp pasta! It's perfect for a quick weeknight dinner or a special occasion meal.

Chicken Stir-fry with Cashews

Ingredients:

- 1 lb (about 450g) boneless, skinless chicken breasts or thighs, cut into bite-sized pieces
- 1/2 cup raw cashews
- 2 tablespoons soy sauce
- 1 tablespoon oyster sauce
- 1 tablespoon hoisin sauce
- 1 tablespoon rice vinegar or white vinegar
- 1 tablespoon cornstarch
- 1 tablespoon water
- 2 tablespoons vegetable oil (for stir-frying)
- 3 cloves garlic, minced
- 1-inch piece of ginger, minced or grated
- 1 bell pepper, sliced (any color you prefer)
- 1 cup snow peas or sugar snap peas, trimmed
- 3-4 green onions, sliced
- Cooked rice, for serving

Instructions:

1. Marinate the chicken:
   - In a bowl, combine the soy sauce, oyster sauce, hoisin sauce, and rice vinegar. Add the chicken pieces and toss to coat. Let it marinate for about 15-20 minutes.
2. Toast the cashews:
   - Heat a dry skillet over medium heat. Add the cashews and toast them, stirring frequently, until they are lightly golden and fragrant. Remove from heat and set aside.
3. Prepare the sauce:
   - In a small bowl, mix together the cornstarch and water to make a slurry.
4. Stir-fry the chicken:
   - Heat 1 tablespoon of vegetable oil in a large skillet or wok over medium-high heat. Add the marinated chicken pieces in a single layer (reserve the marinade). Cook for 3-4 minutes, stirring occasionally, until the chicken is browned and cooked through. Remove the chicken from the skillet and set aside.
5. Cook the vegetables:
   - Add the remaining tablespoon of vegetable oil to the skillet. Add minced garlic and ginger, and stir-fry for about 30 seconds until fragrant.
   - Add the sliced bell pepper and snow peas to the skillet. Stir-fry for 2-3 minutes until the vegetables are crisp-tender.
6. Combine everything:

- Return the cooked chicken to the skillet with the vegetables. Pour in the reserved marinade and the cornstarch slurry. Stir well to coat everything evenly. Cook for another 1-2 minutes until the sauce thickens slightly.
7. Add cashews and green onions:
    - Stir in the toasted cashews and sliced green onions. Toss everything together until well combined and heated through.
8. Serve:
    - Serve the chicken stir-fry with cashews immediately over cooked rice.

Tips:

- Preparation: Have all your ingredients chopped and ready to go before you start cooking, as stir-frying is a quick process.
- Customization: Feel free to add other vegetables such as carrots, broccoli, or mushrooms.
- Sauce consistency: Adjust the thickness of the sauce by adding more or less of the cornstarch slurry.

Enjoy your homemade chicken stir-fry with cashews! It's a flavorful and nutritious dish that's perfect for any day of the week.

One-Pot Chili Mac

Ingredients:

- 1 lb ground beef (you can also use ground turkey or chicken)
- 1 onion, diced
- 3 cloves garlic, minced
- 1 red bell pepper, diced
- 1 can (15 oz) kidney beans, drained and rinsed
- 1 can (15 oz) diced tomatoes
- 1 can (8 oz) tomato sauce
- 2 cups beef broth or chicken broth
- 1 tablespoon chili powder
- 1 teaspoon ground cumin
- 1 teaspoon paprika
- 1/2 teaspoon dried oregano
- Salt and pepper, to taste
- 1 cup elbow macaroni (or any small pasta shape)
- 1 cup shredded cheddar cheese
- Chopped fresh cilantro or green onions, for garnish (optional)
- Sour cream, for serving (optional)

Instructions:

1. Cook the ground beef and vegetables:
   - In a large pot or Dutch oven, cook the ground beef over medium-high heat until browned, breaking it up with a spoon. Drain any excess fat if needed.
   - Add the diced onion, minced garlic, and diced red bell pepper to the pot. Cook for 3-4 minutes until the vegetables are softened.
2. Add beans, tomatoes, and spices:
   - Stir in the drained and rinsed kidney beans, diced tomatoes, tomato sauce, and all the spices (chili powder, cumin, paprika, oregano). Season with salt and pepper to taste.
3. Add broth and pasta:
   - Pour in the beef broth or chicken broth and stir to combine. Bring the mixture to a boil.
4. Cook the pasta:
   - Once boiling, add the elbow macaroni (or pasta of your choice) to the pot. Reduce the heat to medium-low and simmer uncovered for about 10-12 minutes, or until the pasta is cooked al dente and the sauce has thickened, stirring occasionally.
5. Finish and serve:
   - Stir in the shredded cheddar cheese until melted and well combined.
   - Remove the pot from the heat. Taste and adjust seasoning if needed.

- Serve the one-pot chili mac hot, garnished with chopped cilantro or green onions if desired. Offer sour cream on the side for topping.

Tips:

- Variations: Customize your chili mac by adding corn, diced green chilies, or jalapeños for extra heat.
- Storage: Leftovers can be stored in an airtight container in the refrigerator for up to 3-4 days. Reheat gently on the stove or in the microwave, adding a splash of broth or water to loosen the sauce if necessary.
- Make it vegetarian: Skip the ground beef and use additional beans or crumbled tofu for a vegetarian version.

Enjoy your comforting one-pot chili mac! It's perfect for a family meal or a cozy dinner on a chilly evening.

Baked Parmesan Chicken

Ingredients:

- 4 boneless, skinless chicken breasts
- 1 cup breadcrumbs (panko breadcrumbs work well for extra crispiness)
- 1/2 cup grated Parmesan cheese
- 1 teaspoon garlic powder
- 1 teaspoon dried oregano
- 1 teaspoon dried basil
- 1/2 teaspoon paprika
- Salt and pepper, to taste
- 1/2 cup all-purpose flour
- 2 large eggs, beaten
- Cooking spray or olive oil

Instructions:

1. Preheat the oven:
    - Preheat your oven to 400°F (200°C). Lightly grease a baking sheet with cooking spray or olive oil.
2. Prepare the chicken breasts:
    - Pat the chicken breasts dry with paper towels. Season both sides with salt and pepper.
3. Prepare the breading station:
    - Set up three shallow bowls or plates. In the first bowl, place the all-purpose flour. In the second bowl, beat the eggs. In the third bowl, combine the breadcrumbs, grated Parmesan cheese, garlic powder, dried oregano, dried basil, and paprika. Mix well to combine.
4. Bread the chicken:
    - Dredge each chicken breast in the flour, shaking off any excess.
    - Dip the chicken breast into the beaten eggs, allowing any excess to drip off.
    - Press the chicken breast into the breadcrumb mixture, coating both sides evenly and pressing gently to adhere the breadcrumbs.
5. Bake the chicken:
    - Place the breaded chicken breasts on the prepared baking sheet. Lightly spray the tops of the chicken breasts with cooking spray or drizzle with a bit of olive oil for extra crispiness.
    - Bake in the preheated oven for 20-25 minutes, or until the chicken is cooked through and the breadcrumbs are golden brown and crispy. The internal temperature of the chicken should reach 165°F (75°C).
6. Serve:
    - Once baked, remove the chicken breasts from the oven and let them rest for a few minutes before serving. This helps retain their juices.

7. Optional garnish:
   - Garnish with freshly chopped parsley and serve with lemon wedges if desired.

Tips:

- Chicken thickness: If your chicken breasts are thick, you can butterfly them or pound them to an even thickness before breading to ensure even cooking.
- Crispiness: For extra crispy chicken, you can place a wire rack on top of the baking sheet and bake the chicken on the rack. This allows air to circulate around the chicken, crisping up the breadcrumbs on all sides.
- Side dishes: Serve baked Parmesan chicken with a side of roasted vegetables, mashed potatoes, or a fresh salad.

Enjoy your homemade baked Parmesan chicken! It's a crowd-pleasing dish that's perfect for any day of the week.

Teriyaki Salmon

Ingredients:

- 4 salmon fillets (about 6 oz each), skin-on or skinless
- 1/4 cup soy sauce (use low sodium if preferred)
- 1/4 cup mirin (Japanese sweet rice wine)
- 1/4 cup water
- 2 tablespoons brown sugar (or honey)
- 2 cloves garlic, minced
- 1 teaspoon grated fresh ginger (or 1/2 teaspoon ground ginger)
- 1 tablespoon cornstarch
- 1 tablespoon water
- Optional garnish: sliced green onions and sesame seeds

Instructions:

1. Prepare the teriyaki sauce:
    - In a small saucepan, combine soy sauce, mirin, water, brown sugar (or honey), minced garlic, and grated ginger. Bring to a simmer over medium heat, stirring occasionally, until the sugar has dissolved.
2. Thicken the sauce (optional step):
    - In a small bowl, mix cornstarch with 1 tablespoon of water to make a slurry. Slowly pour the cornstarch slurry into the simmering sauce while stirring continuously. Cook for another minute or until the sauce thickens slightly. Remove from heat and set aside.
3. Marinate the salmon:
    - Place the salmon fillets in a shallow dish or a resealable plastic bag. Pour half of the teriyaki sauce over the salmon, reserving the other half for later. Marinate the salmon in the refrigerator for at least 15-30 minutes.
4. Preheat the oven and prepare baking sheet:
    - Preheat your oven to 400°F (200°C). Line a baking sheet with parchment paper or foil and lightly grease with oil or cooking spray.
5. Bake the salmon:
    - Place the marinated salmon fillets on the prepared baking sheet, skin-side down if using skin-on fillets. Bake in the preheated oven for 12-15 minutes, depending on the thickness of the fillets, or until the salmon is cooked through and flakes easily with a fork.
6. Glaze the salmon:
    - While the salmon is baking, pour the reserved teriyaki sauce into a small saucepan. Bring to a simmer over medium heat and cook for a few minutes until slightly thickened.
7. Serve:

- Once the salmon is done, brush or drizzle the thickened teriyaki sauce over the cooked salmon fillets. Garnish with sliced green onions and sesame seeds if desired.

Tips:

- Grilling option: You can also grill the teriyaki salmon instead of baking it. Preheat your grill to medium-high heat and grill the salmon for about 4-5 minutes per side, brushing with the teriyaki sauce during grilling.
- Adjust sweetness: If you prefer a sweeter teriyaki sauce, add more brown sugar or honey to taste.
- Serve with: Teriyaki salmon pairs well with steamed rice and stir-fried vegetables, or a fresh salad for a lighter meal.

Enjoy your delicious homemade teriyaki salmon! It's a perfect dish for a quick and flavorful dinner.

Creamy Tomato Basil Soup

Ingredients:

- 2 tablespoons olive oil
- 1 onion, chopped
- 2 cloves garlic, minced
- 2 tablespoons tomato paste
- 1 can (28 oz) whole peeled tomatoes
- 1 teaspoon sugar (optional, to balance acidity)
- 1 teaspoon dried basil (or 1 tablespoon fresh basil, chopped)
- 1/2 teaspoon dried oregano
- 2 cups vegetable or chicken broth
- 1/2 cup heavy cream (or half-and-half)
- Salt and pepper, to taste
- Fresh basil leaves, for garnish
- Grated Parmesan cheese, for garnish (optional)
- Croutons or crusty bread, for serving (optional)

Instructions:

1. Sauté onion and garlic:
    - Heat olive oil in a large pot or Dutch oven over medium heat. Add chopped onion and sauté until softened, about 5 minutes. Add minced garlic and cook for another 1-2 minutes until fragrant.
2. Add tomato paste and tomatoes:
    - Stir in tomato paste and cook for 1-2 minutes to caramelize slightly. Add the whole peeled tomatoes with their juices. Use a spoon to break up the tomatoes into smaller pieces.
3. Season and simmer:
    - Add sugar (if using), dried basil, and dried oregano. Season with salt and pepper to taste. Stir well to combine.
    - Pour in the vegetable or chicken broth. Bring the mixture to a simmer and cook for about 15-20 minutes, stirring occasionally, to allow the flavors to meld together.
4. Blend the soup:
    - Remove the pot from heat. Use an immersion blender to blend the soup until smooth and creamy. Alternatively, carefully transfer the soup in batches to a blender and blend until smooth, then return to the pot.
5. Add cream:
    - Stir in the heavy cream (or half-and-half) until well combined. Taste and adjust seasoning if needed.
6. Serve:

- Ladle the creamy tomato basil soup into bowls. Garnish each serving with fresh basil leaves and grated Parmesan cheese, if desired. Serve with croutons or crusty bread on the side.

Tips:

- Fresh tomatoes: If you prefer to use fresh tomatoes, you can substitute about 2 lbs of fresh tomatoes (peeled and chopped) for the canned tomatoes.
- Make it vegetarian: Use vegetable broth instead of chicken broth to keep the soup vegetarian.
- Storage: Store leftover soup in an airtight container in the refrigerator for up to 3-4 days. Reheat gently on the stove, adding a splash of broth or cream if needed to adjust consistency.

This creamy tomato basil soup is a comforting and satisfying meal on its own or paired with your favorite sandwiches or salads. Enjoy making and savoring this homemade soup!

Veggie Fried Rice

Ingredients:

- 3 cups cooked rice (preferably chilled, such as leftover rice)
- 2 tablespoons sesame oil or vegetable oil
- 2 cloves garlic, minced
- 1 tablespoon grated ginger
- 1 onion, finely chopped
- 2 carrots, diced
- 1 bell pepper (any color), diced
- 1 cup frozen peas
- 2-3 green onions, chopped
- 2-3 tablespoons soy sauce (adjust to taste)
- 1 tablespoon oyster sauce (optional)
- 1 tablespoon rice vinegar or white vinegar (optional)
- Salt and pepper, to taste
- 2 eggs, lightly beaten (optional)
- Sesame seeds, for garnish (optional)
- Chopped cilantro or parsley, for garnish (optional)

Instructions:

1. Prepare the ingredients:
    - If using leftover rice, make sure it's chilled. Cold rice works best for fried rice as it's less sticky.
2. Sauté aromatics:
    - Heat sesame oil or vegetable oil in a large skillet or wok over medium-high heat. Add minced garlic and grated ginger, sauté for about 30 seconds until fragrant.
3. Cook vegetables:
    - Add finely chopped onion, diced carrots, and diced bell pepper to the skillet. Stir-fry for 3-4 minutes until vegetables are tender-crisp.
4. Add peas and green onions:
    - Stir in frozen peas and chopped green onions. Cook for another 1-2 minutes until peas are heated through.
5. Make the fried rice:
    - Push the vegetables to one side of the skillet. If using eggs, pour them into the empty space and scramble until cooked through. Once eggs are cooked, mix them with the vegetables.
6. Add rice and sauces:
    - Add the chilled cooked rice to the skillet. Break up any clumps with a spatula and toss everything together.

- Drizzle soy sauce and oyster sauce (if using) over the rice. Add rice vinegar for a bit of tanginess if desired. Mix well to evenly distribute the sauces. Adjust seasoning with salt and pepper to taste.
7. Finish and serve:
    - Continue to stir-fry for another 3-4 minutes, allowing the rice to heat through and absorb the flavors.
    - Remove from heat and garnish with sesame seeds and chopped cilantro or parsley, if desired.
8. Serve hot:
    - Serve veggie fried rice hot as a main dish or side dish. Enjoy on its own or with additional protein such as tofu, chicken, or shrimp.

Tips:

- Customization: Feel free to add other vegetables such as broccoli, corn, mushrooms, or bean sprouts based on your preference.
- Protein options: You can add cooked chicken, shrimp, tofu, or even leftover ham to make it a more substantial meal.
- Storage: Leftover fried rice can be stored in an airtight container in the refrigerator for up to 3-4 days. Reheat gently in a skillet or microwave, adding a splash of soy sauce or broth to refresh the flavors.

Enjoy making this versatile and flavorful veggie fried rice at home! It's a great way to use up leftover rice and vegetables while creating a delicious meal.

BBQ Pulled Pork Sandwiches

Ingredients:

For the Pulled Pork:

- 3-4 lbs pork shoulder (also known as pork butt), boneless
- Salt and pepper, to taste
- 1 tablespoon smoked paprika
- 1 tablespoon garlic powder
- 1 tablespoon onion powder
- 1 teaspoon cayenne pepper (optional, for heat)
- 1 cup chicken broth or water
- 1 cup barbecue sauce, plus extra for serving

For Serving:

- Hamburger buns or sandwich rolls
- Coleslaw (optional, for topping)
- Pickles (optional, for topping)

Instructions:

1. Prepare the Pork:
    - Season the pork shoulder generously with salt, pepper, smoked paprika, garlic powder, onion powder, and cayenne pepper (if using). Rub the seasonings all over the pork.
2. Cook the Pork:
    - Option 1: Slow Cooker Method
        - Place the seasoned pork shoulder in a slow cooker. Pour chicken broth or water around the pork (not over it). Cover and cook on low for 8-10 hours or on high for 4-6 hours, until the pork is very tender and easily shreds with a fork.
        - Remove the pork from the slow cooker and shred it using two forks. Discard any excess fat.
        - Option 2: Oven Method
        - Preheat your oven to 325°F (160°C). Place the seasoned pork shoulder in a roasting pan or Dutch oven. Add chicken broth or water to the pan.
        - Cover the pan tightly with foil or a lid. Roast in the oven for 3-4 hours, or until the pork is very tender and shreds easily with a fork.
        - Remove the pork from the oven and shred it using two forks. Discard any excess fat.
3. Make the BBQ Pulled Pork:
    - Place the shredded pork back into the slow cooker or a large pot if using the oven method. Pour barbecue sauce over the shredded pork and stir to combine.

- Heat the BBQ pulled pork on low heat for another 30 minutes to allow the flavors to meld together.
4. Assemble the Sandwiches:
   - Toast the hamburger buns or sandwich rolls lightly, if desired.
   - Spoon a generous amount of BBQ pulled pork onto the bottom half of each bun.
   - Top with coleslaw and pickles if using.
   - Place the top half of the bun on top of the filling.
5. Serve:
   - Serve the BBQ pulled pork sandwiches immediately, with extra barbecue sauce on the side if desired.

Tips:

- Make ahead: BBQ pulled pork can be made ahead of time and stored in the refrigerator for up to 3 days. Reheat gently on the stove or in the microwave before serving.
- Variations: Customize your sandwiches by adding cheese slices, jalapeños, or sliced red onions for extra flavor and crunch.
- Side dishes: Serve with potato chips, french fries, or a side salad to complete the meal.

Enjoy these delicious and satisfying BBQ pulled pork sandwiches for a hearty meal that's perfect for gatherings or a cozy dinner at home!

Beef and Broccoli Stir-fry

Ingredients:

- For the Beef Marinade:
    - 1 lb (450g) flank steak or sirloin steak, thinly sliced against the grain
    - 2 tablespoons soy sauce
    - 1 tablespoon oyster sauce
    - 1 tablespoon cornstarch
    - 1 teaspoon sesame oil
    - 1 teaspoon grated ginger
    - 2 cloves garlic, minced
    - Freshly ground black pepper
- For the Stir-fry:
    - 1 tablespoon vegetable oil
    - 1 onion, thinly sliced
    - 2 cups broccoli florets
    - 1 red bell pepper, thinly sliced (optional)
    - 1/2 cup beef broth or chicken broth
    - 2 tablespoons soy sauce
    - 1 tablespoon oyster sauce
    - 1 tablespoon hoisin sauce (optional, for added sweetness)
    - 1 teaspoon cornstarch mixed with 2 tablespoons water (for thickening)
    - Salt and pepper, to taste
    - Cooked rice, for serving

Instructions:

1. Marinate the Beef:
    - In a bowl, combine the thinly sliced beef with soy sauce, oyster sauce, cornstarch, sesame oil, grated ginger, minced garlic, and black pepper. Mix well to coat the beef evenly. Let it marinate for at least 15-20 minutes.
2. Prepare the Stir-fry Sauce:
    - In a small bowl, mix together beef broth, soy sauce, oyster sauce, and hoisin sauce (if using). Set aside.
3. Stir-fry the Beef and Vegetables:
    - Heat 1 tablespoon of vegetable oil in a large skillet or wok over medium-high heat. Add the marinated beef in a single layer, reserving the marinade. Stir-fry for 2-3 minutes until the beef is browned and cooked through. Remove the beef from the skillet and set aside.
4. Cook the Vegetables:
    - In the same skillet or wok, add a bit more oil if needed. Add thinly sliced onion, broccoli florets, and red bell pepper (if using). Stir-fry for 3-4 minutes until the vegetables are tender-crisp.

5. Combine Everything:
    - Return the cooked beef to the skillet with the vegetables. Pour in the stir-fry sauce that was set aside earlier. Bring to a simmer.
6. Thicken the Sauce:
    - Stir in the cornstarch-water mixture to the skillet, stirring constantly. Cook for another 1-2 minutes until the sauce thickens and coats the beef and vegetables. Adjust seasoning with salt and pepper to taste.
7. Serve:
    - Serve the beef and broccoli stir-fry hot over cooked rice.

Tips:

- Slicing beef: For tender beef, slice it thinly against the grain. This helps break down the muscle fibers and makes the beef more tender.
- Vegetables: Feel free to add other vegetables like snap peas, mushrooms, or carrots to customize your stir-fry.
- Rice: Serve the beef and broccoli stir-fry over steamed white rice, brown rice, or even noodles if preferred.

Enjoy this homemade beef and broccoli stir-fry, packed with savory flavors and tender beef, for a satisfying meal any day of the week!

Margherita Pizza

Ingredients:

- Pizza Dough:
    - 1 pound (450g) pizza dough, homemade or store-bought
    - Cornmeal or flour, for dusting
- Pizza Sauce:
    - 1/2 cup tomato sauce or crushed tomatoes
    - 1 clove garlic, minced
    - 1/2 teaspoon dried oregano
    - Salt and pepper, to taste
- Toppings:
    - 8 oz (225g) fresh mozzarella cheese, sliced or torn into pieces
    - 1-2 large ripe tomatoes, thinly sliced
    - Fresh basil leaves
    - Extra virgin olive oil, for drizzling
- Optional:
    - Grated Parmesan cheese
    - Red pepper flakes

Instructions:

1. Preheat the Oven:
    - Preheat your oven to the highest temperature possible, typically around 475-500°F (245-260°C). If you have a pizza stone, place it in the oven to preheat as well.
2. Prepare the Pizza Dough:
    - On a lightly floured surface, roll out the pizza dough into a circle or rectangle of about 12 inches (30 cm) in diameter or to your desired thickness. If using store-bought dough, follow package instructions for rolling out.
3. Make the Pizza Sauce:
    - In a small bowl, mix together the tomato sauce or crushed tomatoes with minced garlic, dried oregano, salt, and pepper. Adjust seasoning to taste.
4. Assemble the Pizza:
    - Place the rolled-out pizza dough on a pizza peel or an upside-down baking sheet dusted with cornmeal or flour (this helps prevent sticking).
    - Spread the pizza sauce evenly over the dough, leaving a small border around the edges for the crust.
5. Add Toppings:
    - Arrange the sliced fresh mozzarella cheese evenly over the sauce.
    - Place the thinly sliced tomatoes on top of the cheese.
6. Bake the Pizza:

- Carefully transfer the assembled pizza onto the preheated pizza stone in the oven. If you don't have a pizza stone, you can bake the pizza on a baking sheet.
- Bake for 10-12 minutes, or until the crust is golden brown and the cheese is melted and bubbly.

7. Finish the Pizza:
   - Remove the pizza from the oven and immediately top with fresh basil leaves.
   - Drizzle with extra virgin olive oil and sprinkle with grated Parmesan cheese and red pepper flakes if desired.
8. Serve:
   - Slice the Margherita pizza and serve hot. Enjoy the classic flavors of tomato, fresh mozzarella, and basil!

Tips:

- Pizza dough: If making homemade pizza dough, ensure it's rolled out evenly for a crispy crust.
- Cheese: Use fresh mozzarella for the best texture and flavor. You can also use bocconcini or Fior di Latte.
- Fresh basil: Add basil leaves after baking to retain their vibrant color and fresh flavor.
- Variations: For a twist, you can drizzle balsamic glaze over the pizza before serving or add prosciutto slices for a bit of saltiness.

Enjoy making and savoring this authentic Margherita pizza at home! It's a perfect dish for pizza nights or casual gatherings.

Garlic Butter Shrimp Scampi

Ingredients:

- 1 lb (450g) large shrimp, peeled and deveined
- Salt and pepper, to taste
- 4 tablespoons unsalted butter
- 4 cloves garlic, minced
- 1/4 teaspoon red pepper flakes (adjust to taste)
- 1/4 cup white wine (such as Sauvignon Blanc or Pinot Grigio)
- Juice of 1 lemon (about 2-3 tablespoons)
- 1/4 cup chicken broth or seafood broth
- 1/4 cup chopped fresh parsley
- Cooked pasta, for serving (optional)
- Lemon wedges, for serving
- Grated Parmesan cheese, for serving (optional)
- Chopped fresh parsley, for garnish

Instructions:

1. Prepare the Shrimp:
   - Pat the shrimp dry with paper towels. Season with salt and pepper to taste.
2. Cook the Shrimp:
   - In a large skillet, melt 2 tablespoons of butter over medium-high heat. Add the shrimp in a single layer and cook for about 2 minutes per side, or until shrimp are pink and opaque. Remove shrimp from skillet and set aside.
3. Make the Garlic Butter Sauce:
   - In the same skillet, melt the remaining 2 tablespoons of butter over medium heat. Add minced garlic and red pepper flakes. Cook for about 1 minute, stirring constantly, until garlic is fragrant.
4. Deglaze the Pan:
   - Pour in the white wine and lemon juice, scraping up any browned bits from the bottom of the skillet. Simmer for 2-3 minutes to reduce the liquid slightly.
5. Add Broth and Finish Sauce:
   - Stir in the chicken broth or seafood broth. Simmer for another 1-2 minutes until the sauce is slightly thickened.
6. Combine Shrimp and Sauce:
   - Return the cooked shrimp to the skillet. Toss the shrimp in the garlic butter sauce until well coated. Stir in chopped fresh parsley.
7. Serve:
   - Serve the garlic butter shrimp scampi hot, over cooked pasta if desired.
   - Garnish with additional chopped parsley, lemon wedges, and grated Parmesan cheese if desired.

Tips:

- Wine substitution: If you prefer not to use wine, you can substitute with additional chicken broth or seafood broth.
- Pasta option: Garlic butter shrimp scampi pairs beautifully with pasta such as linguine or spaghetti. Toss the cooked pasta with the shrimp and sauce before serving.
- Garnish: Fresh parsley and grated Parmesan cheese add a burst of flavor and freshness to the dish.

This garlic butter shrimp scampi is perfect for a quick and elegant dinner. Enjoy the rich flavors of garlic, butter, and shrimp in every bite!

Thai Red Curry

Ingredients:

- 1 tablespoon vegetable oil
- 2-3 tablespoons Thai red curry paste (adjust to taste)
- 1 can (14 oz) coconut milk
- 1 cup vegetable or chicken broth
- 1 tablespoon soy sauce (or fish sauce for a more authentic flavor)
- 1 tablespoon brown sugar (optional, adjust to taste)
- 1 red bell pepper, sliced
- 1 yellow bell pepper, sliced
- 1 medium carrot, sliced
- 1 small onion, sliced
- 1 cup broccoli florets
- 1 cup sliced mushrooms (such as button or shiitake)
- 1 lb (450g) protein of choice: sliced chicken, shrimp, tofu, or vegetables like sliced tofu or extra vegetables
- Fresh basil leaves or cilantro, for garnish
- Cooked rice or noodles, for serving

Instructions:

1. Prepare Ingredients:
    - Slice the bell peppers, carrot, onion, broccoli, mushrooms, and prepare your choice of protein (chicken, shrimp, tofu, etc.).
2. Cook the Curry Base:
    - Heat vegetable oil in a large skillet or wok over medium heat. Add Thai red curry paste and stir-fry for 1-2 minutes until fragrant.
3. Add Coconut Milk and Broth:
    - Pour in the coconut milk and vegetable or chicken broth. Stir well to combine and bring to a simmer.
4. Season the Curry:
    - Add soy sauce (or fish sauce) and brown sugar (if using). Stir to combine. Taste and adjust seasoning as needed. The curry should be savory with a hint of sweetness.
5. Cook Vegetables and Protein:
    - Add sliced bell peppers, carrot, onion, broccoli, mushrooms, and your choice of protein to the simmering curry sauce. Cook until vegetables are tender and protein is cooked through, about 8-10 minutes depending on the ingredients used.
6. Finish and Serve:
    - Once vegetables and protein are cooked, remove the curry from heat. Stir in fresh basil leaves or cilantro for added freshness and aroma.

7. Serve:
    - Serve Thai red curry hot over cooked rice or noodles.
    - Garnish with additional fresh basil leaves or cilantro if desired.

Tips:

- Red curry paste: Adjust the amount of Thai red curry paste based on your spice preference. Start with 2 tablespoons for a mild to medium heat level.
- Protein options: Feel free to customize with your favorite protein or keep it vegetarian with tofu and extra vegetables.
- Vegetable variation: Use any vegetables you have on hand or prefer. Thai red curry is versatile and can accommodate a variety of vegetables like zucchini, snap peas, or baby corn.

Enjoy this homemade Thai red curry packed with vibrant flavors and creamy coconut goodness. It's a perfect dish for a cozy dinner at home!

Pesto Pasta with Cherry Tomatoes

Ingredients:

- 12 oz (340g) pasta of your choice (such as spaghetti, fettuccine, or penne)
- 1 cup cherry tomatoes, halved
- 1/2 cup basil pesto (homemade or store-bought)
- 1/4 cup grated Parmesan cheese, plus extra for serving
- Salt and freshly ground black pepper, to taste
- Fresh basil leaves, for garnish (optional)
- Red pepper flakes, for garnish (optional)
- Extra virgin olive oil, for drizzling (optional)

Instructions:

1. Cook the Pasta:
   - Bring a large pot of salted water to a boil. Cook the pasta according to package instructions until al dente. Reserve about 1/2 cup of pasta water before draining.
2. Prepare the Cherry Tomatoes:
   - While the pasta is cooking, halve the cherry tomatoes and set them aside.
3. Combine Pasta and Pesto:
   - Drain the cooked pasta and return it to the pot (off the heat). Add basil pesto and grated Parmesan cheese to the pasta. Toss well to coat the pasta evenly with the pesto. If needed, add a splash of reserved pasta water to loosen the sauce.
4. Add Cherry Tomatoes:
   - Gently fold in the halved cherry tomatoes into the pasta and pesto mixture. The residual heat from the pasta will warm the tomatoes slightly.
5. Season and Serve:
   - Taste and season the pesto pasta with salt and freshly ground black pepper as needed.
6. Garnish and Serve:
   - Divide the pesto pasta with cherry tomatoes among serving plates. Garnish with additional grated Parmesan cheese, fresh basil leaves, and red pepper flakes if desired.
   - Drizzle with a little extra virgin olive oil for added richness (optional).

Tips:

- Pesto variation: You can use traditional basil pesto or try variations like sun-dried tomato pesto or spinach pesto for different flavors.
- Additional toppings: Feel free to add grilled chicken, shrimp, or roasted vegetables to make it a heartier meal.
- Make it creamy: For a creamier sauce, stir in a spoonful of ricotta cheese or cream cheese with the pesto.

- Serve with: Pesto pasta with cherry tomatoes pairs wonderfully with a crisp green salad and crusty bread.

Enjoy this easy and flavorful pesto pasta with cherry tomatoes as a quick and satisfying meal any day of the week!

Turkey Burgers

Ingredients:

- For the Turkey Burgers:
    - 1 lb (450g) ground turkey (preferably a mix of dark and white meat for more moisture)
    - 1/4 cup breadcrumbs
    - 1/4 cup finely chopped onion
    - 1 egg, lightly beaten
    - 2 cloves garlic, minced
    - 2 tablespoons chopped fresh parsley (or 1 tablespoon dried parsley)
    - 1 tablespoon Worcestershire sauce
    - 1 teaspoon Dijon mustard
    - 1/2 teaspoon salt
    - 1/4 teaspoon black pepper
- For Serving:
    - Burger buns
    - Lettuce leaves
    - Sliced tomatoes
    - Sliced red onion
    - Pickles
    - Cheese slices (optional)
    - Condiments: mayonnaise, ketchup, mustard, etc.

Instructions:

1. Prepare the Turkey Burger Mixture:
    - In a large bowl, combine the ground turkey, breadcrumbs, finely chopped onion, beaten egg, minced garlic, chopped parsley, Worcestershire sauce, Dijon mustard, salt, and black pepper. Mix until just combined; avoid over-mixing to keep the burgers tender.
2. Shape the Patties:
    - Divide the mixture into 4 equal portions and shape them into patties, about 1/2 inch thick. Make a slight indentation in the center of each patty with your thumb to prevent them from puffing up during cooking.
3. Cook the Turkey Burgers:
    - Grilling: Preheat your grill to medium-high heat. Lightly oil the grill grates to prevent sticking. Grill the patties for about 5-6 minutes per side, or until the internal temperature reaches 165°F (74°C) and the burgers are no longer pink in the center.
    - Stovetop: Heat a skillet or grill pan over medium-high heat. Add a little oil to the pan to prevent sticking. Cook the patties for about 5-6 minutes per side, or until fully cooked through.

4. Toast the Buns:
    - While the burgers are cooking, you can toast the burger buns on the grill or in a toaster for added texture and flavor.
5. Assemble the Burgers:
    - Place each cooked turkey burger on the bottom half of a toasted bun. Top with lettuce, sliced tomatoes, sliced red onion, pickles, and cheese slices if using.
    - Add your favorite condiments to the top half of the bun and place it on top of the burger.
6. Serve:
    - Serve the turkey burgers hot with your favorite side dishes, such as French fries, sweet potato fries, or a fresh salad.

Tips:

- Moisture: Ground turkey can be lean, so the addition of breadcrumbs and an egg helps to keep the burgers moist and hold their shape.
- Seasonings: Feel free to experiment with different herbs and spices to customize the flavor of your turkey burgers.
- Cheese: If adding cheese, place a slice on each patty during the last minute of cooking and cover to melt.
- Toppings: Customize your burger with additional toppings like avocado, bacon, or sautéed mushrooms for extra flavor.

Enjoy these flavorful and juicy turkey burgers for a healthier yet satisfying meal!

Mushroom Risotto

Ingredients:

- 1 1/2 cups Arborio rice
- 6 cups chicken or vegetable broth, kept warm
- 1/2 cup dry white wine
- 1 lb (450g) mushrooms (such as cremini, shiitake, or button), cleaned and sliced
- 1 small onion, finely chopped
- 2 cloves garlic, minced
- 2 tablespoons olive oil
- 2 tablespoons butter
- 1/2 cup grated Parmesan cheese
- Salt and freshly ground black pepper, to taste
- Fresh parsley or chives, chopped, for garnish (optional)

Instructions:

1. Prepare the Broth:
   - In a saucepan, heat the chicken or vegetable broth and keep it warm over low heat.
2. Cook the Mushrooms:
   - In a large skillet, heat 1 tablespoon of olive oil and 1 tablespoon of butter over medium-high heat. Add the sliced mushrooms and cook until they are browned and tender, about 5-7 minutes. Season with a little salt and pepper. Remove the mushrooms from the skillet and set aside.
3. Sauté the Onions and Garlic:
   - In the same skillet, add the remaining 1 tablespoon of olive oil and 1 tablespoon of butter. Add the chopped onion and sauté until it becomes translucent, about 3-4 minutes. Add the minced garlic and cook for another 1-2 minutes until fragrant.
4. Toast the Rice:
   - Add the Arborio rice to the skillet with the onions and garlic. Stir to coat the rice with the oil and butter. Cook for about 2 minutes, stirring constantly, until the edges of the rice become translucent.
5. Deglaze with Wine:
   - Pour in the white wine and stir until it is fully absorbed by the rice.
6. Add Broth Gradually:
   - Begin adding the warm broth to the rice, one ladleful (about 1/2 cup) at a time. Stir frequently and allow the rice to absorb most of the liquid before adding more. Continue this process until the rice is creamy and cooked to al dente, about 18-20 minutes.
7. Combine and Finish:

        - Once the rice is cooked, stir in the cooked mushrooms. Add the grated Parmesan cheese and stir until melted and well combined. Season with salt and freshly ground black pepper to taste.
8. Garnish and Serve:
        - Remove the skillet from heat and let the risotto sit for a couple of minutes. Garnish with chopped fresh parsley or chives, if desired. Serve the mushroom risotto hot.

Tips:

- Consistency: The key to a perfect risotto is its creamy consistency. The rice should be tender yet slightly firm to the bite (al dente). If you run out of broth and the rice is not yet cooked, you can use warm water.
- Stirring: Frequent stirring helps release the rice's starch, creating the dish's signature creamy texture.
- Mushroom variety: Feel free to use a mix of different mushrooms to add depth of flavor.
- Additional flavors: For an extra flavor boost, you can add a splash of truffle oil before serving or incorporate a handful of sautéed spinach towards the end of cooking.

Enjoy this creamy and delicious mushroom risotto as a comforting main dish or a satisfying side!

Honey Garlic Chicken Thighs

Ingredients:

- 8 bone-in, skin-on chicken thighs
- Salt and freshly ground black pepper, to taste
- 2 tablespoons olive oil
- 1/4 cup honey
- 1/4 cup soy sauce
- 4 cloves garlic, minced
- 1 tablespoon apple cider vinegar or rice vinegar
- 1 teaspoon grated fresh ginger (optional)
- 1/2 teaspoon red pepper flakes (optional, for a bit of heat)
- Fresh parsley or green onions, chopped, for garnish (optional)
- Sesame seeds, for garnish (optional)

Instructions:

1. **Preheat the Oven:**
   - Preheat your oven to 400°F (200°C).
2. **Prepare the Chicken:**
   - Season the chicken thighs generously with salt and freshly ground black pepper on both sides.
3. **Sear the Chicken:**
   - In a large oven-safe skillet, heat the olive oil over medium-high heat. Place the chicken thighs in the skillet, skin-side down, and sear for 5-7 minutes until the skin is crispy and golden brown. Flip the chicken thighs and sear the other side for an additional 3-4 minutes. Remove the chicken from the skillet and set aside.
4. **Make the Sauce:**
   - In the same skillet, lower the heat to medium. Add the minced garlic and cook for about 1 minute until fragrant, being careful not to burn it. Add the honey, soy sauce, vinegar, grated ginger (if using), and red pepper flakes (if using). Stir to combine and let the sauce simmer for 2-3 minutes until slightly thickened.
5. **Combine Chicken and Sauce:**
   - Return the seared chicken thighs to the skillet, skin-side up. Spoon some of the sauce over the chicken thighs.
6. **Bake the Chicken:**
   - Transfer the skillet to the preheated oven. Bake for 25-30 minutes, or until the chicken thighs are fully cooked and reach an internal temperature of 165°F (74°C). Baste the chicken with the sauce halfway through baking.
7. **Serve:**
   - Once the chicken is cooked, remove the skillet from the oven. Let the chicken rest for a few minutes. Garnish with chopped fresh parsley or green onions and sesame seeds if desired.

8. Enjoy:
    - Serve the honey garlic chicken thighs hot, with your favorite sides such as rice, roasted vegetables, or a fresh salad.

Tips:

- Crispy Skin: Searing the chicken thighs before baking helps to achieve a crispy skin. Ensure the skillet is hot enough before adding the chicken.
- Sauce Variation: For a thicker sauce, you can mix 1 teaspoon of cornstarch with 1 tablespoon of water and add it to the sauce before baking.
- Flavor Boost: Add a splash of lemon juice to the sauce for a tangy twist.
- Meal Prep: This dish is great for meal prep. Store the cooked chicken thighs and sauce in an airtight container in the refrigerator for up to 4 days.

Enjoy these flavorful and juicy honey garlic chicken thighs as a delightful main course!

Veggie Quesadillas

Ingredients:

- 4 large flour tortillas
- 1 1/2 cups shredded cheese (such as cheddar, Monterey Jack, or a Mexican blend)
- 1 small red bell pepper, thinly sliced
- 1 small yellow bell pepper, thinly sliced
- 1 small zucchini, thinly sliced
- 1 small red onion, thinly sliced
- 1 cup mushrooms, sliced
- 1 cup corn kernels (fresh, frozen, or canned)
- 1 can (15 oz) black beans, drained and rinsed
- 2 tablespoons olive oil
- 1 teaspoon ground cumin
- 1 teaspoon chili powder
- Salt and pepper, to taste
- Fresh cilantro, chopped (optional)
- Sour cream, salsa, and guacamole, for serving

Instructions:

1. Prepare the Vegetables:
    - Heat 1 tablespoon of olive oil in a large skillet over medium-high heat. Add the sliced bell peppers, zucchini, red onion, and mushrooms. Sauté for about 5-7 minutes until the vegetables are tender.
    - Add the corn and black beans to the skillet. Season with ground cumin, chili powder, salt, and pepper. Cook for an additional 2-3 minutes until everything is well combined and heated through. Remove from heat.
2. Assemble the Quesadillas:
    - Heat a clean, large skillet or griddle over medium heat. Brush one side of a tortilla with a small amount of olive oil and place it oil-side down in the skillet.
    - Sprinkle about 1/4 cup of shredded cheese evenly over half of the tortilla. Spread a generous amount of the veggie mixture over the cheese. Sprinkle another 1/4 cup of cheese over the veggies.
    - Fold the tortilla in half to cover the filling. Press down gently with a spatula.
3. Cook the Quesadillas:
    - Cook for 2-3 minutes on each side, or until the tortilla is golden brown and crispy and the cheese is melted. Adjust the heat as necessary to prevent burning. Repeat with the remaining tortillas and filling.
4. Serve:
    - Cut each quesadilla into wedges and serve hot with sour cream, salsa, and guacamole on the side. Garnish with fresh cilantro if desired.

Tips:

- Vegetable Variety: Feel free to add or substitute other vegetables such as spinach, kale, tomatoes, or avocado.
- Cheese: Using a mix of cheeses can add depth of flavor. Try a combination of cheddar and pepper jack for a bit of a kick.
- Tortilla Options: Whole wheat or gluten-free tortillas can be used as an alternative to regular flour tortillas.
- Make Ahead: The vegetable mixture can be prepared ahead of time and stored in the refrigerator for up to 3 days. Assemble and cook the quesadillas when ready to serve.

Enjoy these flavorful and satisfying veggie quesadillas as a main dish or a tasty appetizer!

Lemon Herb Grilled Chicken

Ingredients:

- 4 boneless, skinless chicken breasts
- 1/4 cup olive oil
- 1/4 cup freshly squeezed lemon juice (about 2 lemons)
- Zest of 1 lemon
- 3 cloves garlic, minced
- 1 tablespoon chopped fresh rosemary (or 1 teaspoon dried rosemary)
- 1 tablespoon chopped fresh thyme (or 1 teaspoon dried thyme)
- 1 tablespoon chopped fresh parsley (optional)
- 1 teaspoon Dijon mustard
- Salt and freshly ground black pepper, to taste
- Lemon slices, for garnish (optional)
- Fresh herbs, for garnish (optional)

Instructions:

1. Prepare the Marinade:
   - In a small bowl, whisk together the olive oil, lemon juice, lemon zest, minced garlic, chopped rosemary, chopped thyme, chopped parsley (if using), Dijon mustard, salt, and pepper.
2. Marinate the Chicken:
   - Place the chicken breasts in a resealable plastic bag or a shallow dish. Pour the marinade over the chicken, making sure each piece is well coated. Seal the bag or cover the dish and refrigerate for at least 30 minutes to 2 hours. For the best flavor, marinate for up to 4 hours. Do not marinate for more than 8 hours as the acid from the lemon can begin to "cook" the chicken and affect its texture.
3. Preheat the Grill:
   - Preheat your grill to medium-high heat (about 400°F / 200°C). If using a charcoal grill, make sure the coals are evenly distributed and glowing red with a light ash coating.
4. Grill the Chicken:
   - Remove the chicken breasts from the marinade, letting any excess drip off. Discard the marinade.
   - Place the chicken on the preheated grill. Grill for about 6-8 minutes per side, or until the chicken is cooked through and has an internal temperature of 165°F (74°C). Cooking times may vary depending on the thickness of the chicken breasts.
5. Rest and Serve:
   - Remove the chicken from the grill and let it rest for a few minutes to allow the juices to redistribute.
   - Garnish with lemon slices and fresh herbs if desired. Serve hot.

Tips:

- Pound the Chicken: For even cooking, pound the chicken breasts to an even thickness before marinating. This helps ensure that the chicken cooks evenly and stays juicy.
- Indoor Cooking: If you don't have a grill, you can cook the chicken on a stovetop grill pan or bake it in the oven at 400°F (200°C) for about 20-25 minutes, or until fully cooked.
- Side Dishes: Lemon herb grilled chicken pairs wonderfully with a variety of sides such as grilled vegetables, a fresh salad, quinoa, or rice.
- Leftovers: Use leftover grilled chicken in salads, sandwiches, or wraps for a delicious meal the next day.

Enjoy this fresh and zesty lemon herb grilled chicken as a delightful and healthy main course!

Sausage and Peppers

Ingredients:

- 1 1/2 lbs (about 6) Italian sausages (sweet, mild, or hot according to preference)
- 2 tablespoons olive oil
- 1 large onion, thinly sliced
- 1 red bell pepper, thinly sliced
- 1 yellow bell pepper, thinly sliced
- 1 green bell pepper, thinly sliced
- 3 cloves garlic, minced
- 1/2 cup crushed tomatoes or tomato sauce
- 1/2 cup chicken broth
- 1 teaspoon dried oregano
- 1 teaspoon dried basil
- 1/2 teaspoon red pepper flakes (optional, for added heat)
- Salt and freshly ground black pepper, to taste
- Fresh basil or parsley, chopped, for garnish (optional)
- Crusty bread or rolls, for serving (optional)

Instructions:

1. Cook the Sausages:
    - In a large skillet or sauté pan, heat 1 tablespoon of olive oil over medium-high heat. Add the sausages and cook until browned on all sides, about 5-7 minutes. Remove the sausages from the skillet and set aside. They do not need to be fully cooked at this stage.
2. Sauté the Vegetables:
    - In the same skillet, add the remaining 1 tablespoon of olive oil. Add the sliced onions and bell peppers. Sauté for about 5-7 minutes, until the vegetables are softened and starting to brown.
3. Add Garlic and Seasonings:
    - Add the minced garlic to the skillet and cook for about 1 minute, until fragrant. Stir in the crushed tomatoes or tomato sauce, chicken broth, dried oregano, dried basil, red pepper flakes (if using), salt, and pepper.
4. Combine Sausages and Vegetables:
    - Return the browned sausages to the skillet, nestling them among the vegetables. Reduce the heat to medium-low, cover, and simmer for about 15-20 minutes, or until the sausages are cooked through (internal temperature of 160°F / 71°C) and the sauce has thickened slightly.
5. Garnish and Serve:
    - If desired, garnish with chopped fresh basil or parsley. Serve the sausage and peppers hot, either on their own or with crusty bread or rolls.

Tips:

- Variations: Feel free to use different types of sausages (e.g., turkey or chicken sausages) or add other vegetables like mushrooms or zucchini.
- Serving Suggestions: Sausage and peppers can be served over pasta, rice, or polenta. They are also delicious served in a hoagie roll as a sandwich.
- Leftovers: Store any leftovers in an airtight container in the refrigerator for up to 3 days. Reheat gently on the stovetop or in the microwave before serving.

Enjoy this savory and satisfying sausage and peppers dish for a comforting meal that's bursting with flavor!

Caprese Salad

Ingredients:

- 4 large ripe tomatoes
- 1 lb fresh mozzarella cheese
- 1 bunch fresh basil leaves
- Extra virgin olive oil
- Balsamic vinegar (optional)
- Sea salt
- Freshly ground black pepper

Instructions:

1. Prepare the Ingredients:
   - Slice the tomatoes and mozzarella cheese into 1/4-inch thick slices.
   - Wash the basil leaves and pat them dry.
2. Arrange the Salad:
   - On a large serving platter, alternate slices of tomato and mozzarella, arranging them in a circle or in rows.
   - Tuck whole basil leaves in between the tomato and mozzarella slices.
3. Season and Dress:
   - Drizzle extra virgin olive oil over the salad.
   - If desired, add a drizzle of balsamic vinegar for extra flavor.
   - Sprinkle sea salt and freshly ground black pepper over the top to taste.
4. Serve:
   - Serve immediately, or chill for a short time before serving to allow the flavors to meld.

Tips:

- Use the freshest, highest quality ingredients you can find, as this salad relies on the flavors of the raw ingredients.
- If you like, you can add a bit of crushed garlic to the olive oil before drizzling it over the salad for an extra kick.
- For a more modern twist, consider adding a few drops of balsamic glaze instead of balsamic vinegar.

Enjoy your Caprese Salad as a refreshing appetizer, side dish, or even a light main course!

Pan-seared Scallops

Ingredients:

- 1 lb large sea scallops
- Salt
- Freshly ground black pepper
- 2 tablespoons olive oil (or a combination of olive oil and butter)
- 2 cloves garlic, minced (optional)
- 1 tablespoon fresh lemon juice
- Fresh parsley, chopped (optional, for garnish)
- Lemon wedges (for serving)

Instructions:

1. Prepare the Scallops:
   - Pat the scallops dry with paper towels. Moisture on the scallops will prevent them from searing properly.
   - Season both sides of the scallops with salt and freshly ground black pepper.
2. Heat the Pan:
   - Heat a large skillet over medium-high heat. Add the olive oil (and butter if using) and heat until shimmering but not smoking.
3. Sear the Scallops:
   - Carefully place the scallops in the hot pan, leaving space between each one to ensure they cook evenly and sear properly.
   - Cook without moving them for about 2-3 minutes on the first side, until a golden-brown crust forms.
4. Flip and Finish Cooking:
   - Using tongs, flip the scallops to the other side and cook for another 1-2 minutes. The scallops should be opaque in the center and have a golden crust on both sides.
   - If using garlic, add it to the pan in the last minute of cooking and sauté briefly, making sure it doesn't burn.
5. Add Lemon Juice:
   - Squeeze fresh lemon juice over the scallops just before removing them from the pan for a bright, fresh flavor.
6. Serve:
   - Transfer the scallops to a serving plate.
   - Garnish with chopped fresh parsley if desired.
   - Serve immediately with lemon wedges on the side.

Tips:

- Ensure your pan is hot before adding the scallops to get a good sear.

- Do not overcrowd the pan; if necessary, sear the scallops in batches.
- For extra flavor, you can deglaze the pan with a splash of white wine or broth after removing the scallops and drizzle the reduction over them before serving.

Enjoy your pan-seared scallops with a side of your choice, such as a fresh salad, steamed vegetables, or a creamy risotto!

Cajun Jambalaya

Ingredients:

- 2 tablespoons vegetable oil
- 1 pound chicken thighs or breasts, cut into bite-sized pieces
- 1 pound Andouille sausage, sliced
- 1 large onion, finely chopped
- 1 green bell pepper, finely chopped
- 2 celery stalks, finely chopped
- 4 cloves garlic, minced
- 1 can (14.5 oz) diced tomatoes
- 2 cups chicken broth
- 1 cup long-grain white rice
- 1 teaspoon dried thyme
- 1 teaspoon dried oregano
- 2 teaspoons Cajun seasoning
- 1/2 teaspoon paprika
- 1/4 teaspoon cayenne pepper (optional, for extra heat)
- 2 bay leaves
- Salt and freshly ground black pepper to taste
- 1 pound shrimp, peeled and deveined
- 2 green onions, sliced (for garnish)
- Fresh parsley, chopped (for garnish)

Instructions:

1. Brown the Meat:
    - Heat the vegetable oil in a large, heavy-bottomed pot or Dutch oven over medium-high heat.
    - Add the chicken pieces and cook until browned on all sides. Remove the chicken and set aside.
    - In the same pot, add the sliced Andouille sausage and cook until browned. Remove and set aside with the chicken.
2. Cook the Vegetables:
    - In the same pot, add the chopped onion, bell pepper, and celery. Cook until the vegetables are softened, about 5-7 minutes.
    - Add the minced garlic and cook for another minute until fragrant.
3. Combine Ingredients:
    - Return the browned chicken and sausage to the pot.
    - Stir in the diced tomatoes (with their juices), chicken broth, and rice.
    - Add the dried thyme, oregano, Cajun seasoning, paprika, cayenne pepper (if using), bay leaves, salt, and black pepper. Stir to combine.
4. Simmer the Jambalaya:

- Bring the mixture to a boil, then reduce the heat to low. Cover the pot and let it simmer for about 25-30 minutes, or until the rice is cooked and has absorbed most of the liquid. Stir occasionally to prevent sticking.
5. Add the Shrimp:
    - Once the rice is cooked, add the peeled and deveined shrimp to the pot. Stir to combine, then cover and cook for another 5-7 minutes, or until the shrimp are pink and cooked through.
6. Finish and Serve:
    - Remove the bay leaves from the pot.
    - Taste and adjust the seasoning with additional salt and pepper if needed.
    - Garnish with sliced green onions and chopped fresh parsley.

Tips:

- For a smokier flavor, you can add a few dashes of smoked paprika.
- If you prefer, you can use a mix of chicken broth and seafood stock for a richer flavor.
- For a milder dish, reduce or omit the cayenne pepper.

Enjoy your Cajun Jambalaya with a side of crusty bread or a simple green salad for a complete meal!

Mediterranean Couscous Salad

Ingredients:

For the Salad:

- 1 cup couscous
- 1 1/4 cups vegetable or chicken broth (or water)
- 1 cucumber, diced
- 1 pint cherry tomatoes, halved
- 1/2 red onion, finely chopped
- 1/2 cup Kalamata olives, sliced
- 1/2 cup crumbled feta cheese
- 1/4 cup chopped fresh parsley
- 1/4 cup chopped fresh mint (optional)
- Salt and freshly ground black pepper, to taste

For the Dressing:

- 1/4 cup extra virgin olive oil
- 2 tablespoons red wine vinegar
- 1 tablespoon lemon juice
- 1 garlic clove, minced
- 1 teaspoon dried oregano
- 1/2 teaspoon Dijon mustard
- Salt and freshly ground black pepper, to taste

Instructions:

1. Cook the Couscous:
    - In a medium saucepan, bring the vegetable or chicken broth to a boil.
    - Stir in the couscous, cover the saucepan with a lid, and remove it from the heat.
    - Let the couscous sit covered for about 5 minutes, allowing it to absorb the broth. Fluff the couscous with a fork to separate the grains and let it cool to room temperature.
2. Prepare the Vegetables and Herbs:
    - While the couscous is cooking, prepare the cucumber, cherry tomatoes, red onion, Kalamata olives, parsley, and mint (if using). Combine them in a large mixing bowl.
3. Make the Dressing:
    - In a small bowl, whisk together the extra virgin olive oil, red wine vinegar, lemon juice, minced garlic, dried oregano, Dijon mustard, salt, and black pepper until well combined.
4. Combine Everything:
    - Add the cooled couscous to the bowl with the vegetables and herbs.

- Pour the dressing over the salad and toss gently to combine, ensuring everything is evenly coated with the dressing.
5. Add Feta Cheese and Season:
    - Gently fold in the crumbled feta cheese.
    - Taste the salad and adjust the seasoning with salt and pepper if needed.
6. Chill and Serve:
    - Cover the salad and refrigerate for at least 30 minutes to allow the flavors to meld together.
    - Serve chilled or at room temperature. Garnish with additional parsley or mint leaves if desired.

Tips:

- You can customize this salad by adding other Mediterranean ingredients such as roasted red peppers, artichoke hearts, or pine nuts.
- To make it a complete meal, add grilled chicken, shrimp, or chickpeas for added protein.
- This salad keeps well in the refrigerator for a few days, making it perfect for meal prep or a picnic.

Enjoy this Mediterranean Couscous Salad as a side dish, light lunch, or a refreshing addition to any summer gathering!

Orange Glazed Pork Chops

Ingredients:

- 4 bone-in pork chops, about 1-inch thick
- Salt and freshly ground black pepper, to taste
- 2 tablespoons olive oil
- 1/2 cup chicken broth
- 1/2 cup freshly squeezed orange juice (about 2 oranges)
- Zest of 1 orange
- 2 tablespoons honey
- 1 tablespoon soy sauce (or tamari for gluten-free)
- 1 teaspoon Dijon mustard
- 2 cloves garlic, minced
- 1 tablespoon cornstarch (optional, for thickening the sauce)
- 2 tablespoons water (optional, for cornstarch slurry)
- Fresh parsley, chopped, for garnish (optional)

Instructions:

1. **Season and Sear the Pork Chops:**
   - Pat the pork chops dry with paper towels and season both sides generously with salt and black pepper.
   - Heat olive oil in a large skillet over medium-high heat.
   - Add the pork chops to the skillet and sear for about 4-5 minutes on each side, or until nicely browned and cooked through (internal temperature should reach 145°F or 63°C). Remove pork chops from the skillet and set aside.
2. **Make the Orange Glaze:**
   - In the same skillet, reduce the heat to medium. Add chicken broth, orange juice, orange zest, honey, soy sauce, Dijon mustard, and minced garlic.
   - Stir well to combine and scrape up any browned bits from the bottom of the skillet.
3. **Simmer and Thicken the Sauce (if desired):**
   - Bring the sauce to a simmer and let it cook for 5-7 minutes, or until slightly thickened.
   - If you prefer a thicker sauce, mix 1 tablespoon of cornstarch with 2 tablespoons of water to make a slurry. Stir the slurry into the simmering sauce and cook for another 1-2 minutes until thickened.
4. **Glaze the Pork Chops:**
   - Return the pork chops to the skillet and spoon the orange glaze over them.
   - Cook for another 1-2 minutes, or until the pork chops are heated through and nicely glazed with the sauce.
5. **Serve:**
   - Transfer the glazed pork chops to a serving platter or individual plates.

- Spoon extra sauce over the pork chops.
- Garnish with chopped fresh parsley, if desired.

Tips:

- Use bone-in pork chops for more flavor, but you can also use boneless if preferred.
- Adjust the sweetness of the glaze by adding more or less honey to suit your taste.
- Serve the orange glazed pork chops with sides like roasted vegetables, mashed potatoes, or a simple green salad.

Enjoy these succulent orange glazed pork chops for a delicious dinner that's sure to impress!

Ratatouille

Ingredients:

- 1 large eggplant, diced
- 2 zucchinis, diced
- 1 yellow bell pepper, diced
- 1 red bell pepper, diced
- 1 onion, diced
- 4 cloves garlic, minced
- 4 tomatoes, diced (or 1 can (14 oz) diced tomatoes)
- 2 tablespoons tomato paste
- 2 tablespoons olive oil
- 1 teaspoon dried thyme
- 1 teaspoon dried oregano
- 1 bay leaf
- Salt and freshly ground black pepper, to taste
- Fresh basil leaves, chopped, for garnish

Instructions:

1. Prepare the Vegetables:
   - Heat 1 tablespoon of olive oil in a large skillet or Dutch oven over medium heat.
   - Add the diced eggplant and cook for about 5 minutes, stirring occasionally, until softened and lightly browned. Remove from the skillet and set aside.
2. Sauté the Onions and Peppers:
   - In the same skillet, add the remaining tablespoon of olive oil.
   - Add the diced onion and bell peppers. Cook for about 5-7 minutes until softened.
3. Add Garlic and Tomatoes:
   - Stir in the minced garlic and cook for another minute until fragrant.
   - Add the diced tomatoes (or canned tomatoes) and tomato paste to the skillet. Stir well to combine.
4. Combine and Simmer:
   - Return the cooked eggplant to the skillet.
   - Add the diced zucchinis, dried thyme, dried oregano, bay leaf, salt, and black pepper. Stir gently to combine all the ingredients.
5. Cook the Ratatouille:
   - Reduce the heat to low and cover the skillet. Let the ratatouille simmer for about 20-30 minutes, stirring occasionally, until all the vegetables are tender and the flavors have melded together.
   - Taste and adjust seasoning if needed.
6. Serve:
   - Remove the bay leaf from the ratatouille.
   - Serve hot, warm, or at room temperature.

- Garnish with chopped fresh basil leaves before serving.

Tips:

- Ratatouille is delicious on its own as a vegetarian main dish, but it can also be served as a side dish with grilled meats or fish.
- You can customize the vegetables based on what you have available or prefer. For example, you can add mushrooms or yellow squash.
- Leftover ratatouille can be stored in the refrigerator for up to 3-4 days and reheated gently on the stove or in the microwave.

Enjoy this comforting and flavorful ratatouille as a taste of French countryside cooking!

Beef and Bean Burritos

Ingredients:

- 1 lb ground beef
- 1 small onion, finely chopped
- 2 cloves garlic, minced
- 1 can (15 oz) black beans, drained and rinsed
- 1 teaspoon ground cumin
- 1 teaspoon chili powder
- 1/2 teaspoon paprika
- Salt and freshly ground black pepper, to taste
- 1 cup shredded cheddar cheese (or your favorite cheese)
- 4 large flour tortillas (burrito-sized)
- Optional toppings: salsa, sour cream, guacamole, chopped tomatoes, shredded lettuce, chopped cilantro

Instructions:

1. Cook the Beef and Onion:
   - In a large skillet, cook the ground beef over medium-high heat until browned and cooked through, breaking it up with a spoon as it cooks.
   - Add the chopped onion and minced garlic to the skillet. Cook for another 2-3 minutes until the onion is softened and translucent.
2. Add Beans and Seasonings:
   - Stir in the black beans, ground cumin, chili powder, paprika, salt, and black pepper. Mix well to combine.
   - Let the mixture simmer for about 5 minutes, stirring occasionally, to allow the flavors to meld together.
   - Taste and adjust seasoning if needed.
3. Prepare the Tortillas:
   - Warm the flour tortillas in a microwave or in a dry skillet for about 10-15 seconds on each side to make them more pliable.
4. Assemble the Burritos:
   - Divide the beef and bean mixture evenly among the tortillas, placing it in a line down the center of each tortilla.
   - Sprinkle shredded cheese over the beef and bean mixture.
5. Fold the Burritos:
   - Fold the sides of each tortilla over the filling, then fold the bottom edge over the filling and roll it up tightly to enclose the filling.
6. Serve:
   - Place the rolled burritos seam-side down on a serving plate.
   - Serve immediately with your choice of toppings such as salsa, sour cream, guacamole, chopped tomatoes, shredded lettuce, and chopped cilantro.

Tips:

- You can customize these burritos by adding rice, sautéed bell peppers, or corn to the filling.
- If you prefer spicier burritos, add a pinch of cayenne pepper or use a spicier salsa.
- To make ahead, you can assemble the burritos, wrap them individually in foil, and store them in the refrigerator or freezer. Reheat in the oven or microwave before serving.

Enjoy these delicious beef and bean burritos with your favorite toppings for a satisfying and flavorful meal!

Garlic Butter Steak Bites

Ingredients:

- 1 lb sirloin steak, cut into bite-sized cubes
- Salt and freshly ground black pepper, to taste
- 2 tablespoons olive oil
- 4 tablespoons unsalted butter
- 4 cloves garlic, minced
- 1 tablespoon chopped fresh parsley (optional, for garnish)

Instructions:

1. Prepare the Steak:
   - Pat the steak cubes dry with paper towels. This helps in achieving a good sear.
   - Season the steak generously with salt and freshly ground black pepper.
2. Sear the Steak:
   - Heat the olive oil in a large skillet over medium-high heat until hot but not smoking.
   - Add the steak cubes in a single layer, making sure not to overcrowd the skillet (you may need to cook in batches). Sear for about 2-3 minutes per side, or until browned and cooked to your desired doneness. Remove the steak from the skillet and set aside.
3. Make the Garlic Butter Sauce:
   - Reduce the heat to medium-low and add the butter to the same skillet.
   - Once the butter is melted, add the minced garlic. Cook for about 1-2 minutes, stirring constantly, until the garlic is fragrant and lightly golden.
4. Combine and Serve:
   - Return the seared steak bites to the skillet with the garlic butter sauce. Toss gently to coat the steak evenly with the sauce.
   - Cook for another minute or so, allowing the flavors to meld together.
   - Remove from heat and garnish with chopped fresh parsley, if desired.
5. Serve:
   - Transfer the garlic butter steak bites to a serving platter or individual plates.
   - Serve immediately as a main course with sides like mashed potatoes, steamed vegetables, or a crisp salad.

Tips:

- For best results, use a skillet that retains heat well, such as cast iron, to get a good sear on the steak.
- Adjust the cooking time depending on how you prefer your steak cooked (rare, medium-rare, medium, etc.).

- You can customize the seasoning by adding herbs like thyme or rosemary to the garlic butter sauce.
- Leftovers can be stored in an airtight container in the refrigerator for a few days and reheated gently on the stove or in the microwave.

Enjoy these tender and flavorful garlic butter steak bites for a delicious meal that's sure to impress!

Chicken Caesar Salad Wraps

Ingredients:

- 2 cups cooked chicken breast, shredded or diced
- 1/2 cup Caesar salad dressing (homemade or store-bought)
- 1/4 cup grated Parmesan cheese
- 1 cup cherry tomatoes, halved
- 2 cups romaine lettuce, chopped
- 4 large flour tortillas (burrito-sized)
- Salt and freshly ground black pepper, to taste

Instructions:

1. Prepare the Chicken:
    - If you haven't already cooked the chicken, you can grill, bake, or pan-sear chicken breasts until fully cooked. Let them cool slightly, then shred or dice into bite-sized pieces.
2. Mix the Salad Ingredients:
    - In a large bowl, combine the shredded or diced chicken with Caesar salad dressing. Toss well to coat the chicken evenly.
    - Add the grated Parmesan cheese, cherry tomatoes, and chopped romaine lettuce to the bowl. Season with salt and freshly ground black pepper to taste. Toss again to combine all the ingredients.
3. Assemble the Wraps:
    - Lay out the flour tortillas on a clean surface.
    - Divide the chicken Caesar salad mixture evenly among the tortillas, placing it in a line down the center of each tortilla.
4. Roll the Wraps:
    - Fold the sides of each tortilla over the filling, then fold the bottom edge over the filling and roll it up tightly to enclose the filling.
5. Serve:
    - Slice the wraps in half diagonally, if desired, and serve immediately.

Tips:

- You can customize these wraps by adding additional ingredients such as crispy bacon bits, croutons, or avocado slices.
- For a lighter version, you can use whole wheat or spinach tortillas.
- If preparing ahead, store the salad mixture separately from the tortillas and assemble just before serving to prevent the tortillas from becoming soggy.

These Chicken Caesar Salad Wraps are perfect for a quick lunch, picnic, or light dinner. They're portable, flavorful, and packed with protein and veggies!

Tomato Basil Bruschetta

Ingredients:

- 4-5 ripe tomatoes, diced
- 1/4 cup fresh basil leaves, thinly sliced (chiffonade)
- 2 cloves garlic, minced
- 2 tablespoons extra virgin olive oil
- 1 tablespoon balsamic vinegar (optional)
- Salt and freshly ground black pepper, to taste
- 1 baguette or Italian bread, sliced into 1/2-inch thick slices
- Olive oil, for brushing on bread
- Optional: 1/4 cup grated Parmesan cheese for topping

Instructions:

1. Prepare the Tomato Basil Mixture:
    - In a medium bowl, combine the diced tomatoes, sliced basil, minced garlic, extra virgin olive oil, and balsamic vinegar (if using).
    - Season with salt and freshly ground black pepper to taste. Mix well to combine all the flavors.
    - Let the mixture sit at room temperature for about 15-20 minutes to allow the flavors to meld together.
2. Toast the Bread:
    - Preheat the oven to 400°F (200°C).
    - Arrange the bread slices on a baking sheet in a single layer.
    - Lightly brush or drizzle olive oil over each slice of bread.
3. Bake the Bread:
    - Bake the bread slices in the preheated oven for about 8-10 minutes, or until they are crispy and lightly golden brown. Keep an eye on them to prevent burning.
    - Alternatively, you can grill the bread slices on a grill pan or outdoor grill until they are toasted and have grill marks.
4. Assemble the Bruschetta:
    - Once the bread slices are toasted, remove them from the oven or grill and let them cool slightly.
    - Spoon a generous amount of the tomato basil mixture onto each slice of toasted bread.
    - Optionally, sprinkle grated Parmesan cheese on top of each bruschetta for added flavor.
5. Serve:
    - Arrange the Tomato Basil Bruschetta on a serving platter.
    - Serve immediately as a delicious appetizer or snack.

Tips:

- Variations: Add a drizzle of balsamic glaze or a few slices of fresh mozzarella cheese on top of each bruschetta for a different twist.
- Storage: If you have leftover tomato basil mixture, store it in an airtight container in the refrigerator. It will keep well for a day or two, and you can use it as a topping for grilled chicken, pasta, or as a fresh salsa for fish.
- Presentation: For a more elegant presentation, you can cut the bread slices diagonally to create smaller, bite-sized bruschetta pieces.

This Tomato Basil Bruschetta recipe is simple yet bursting with fresh flavors, making it a perfect appetizer for any occasion or a light meal on its own. Enjoy the vibrant taste of summer with each bite!

Pad Thai

Ingredients:

For the Pad Thai Sauce:

- 3 tablespoons tamarind paste
- 3 tablespoons fish sauce
- 2 tablespoons soy sauce
- 2 tablespoons brown sugar
- 1 tablespoon rice vinegar
- 1/2 teaspoon chili flakes (adjust to taste)
- 1/4 cup water

For the Pad Thai:

- 8 oz (about 225g) dried rice noodles
- 2 tablespoons vegetable oil
- 1 block firm tofu, cut into small cubes (or substitute with shrimp or chicken)
- 4 cloves garlic, minced
- 2 eggs, lightly beaten
- 1 cup bean sprouts
- 4 green onions, sliced
- 1/2 cup chopped roasted peanuts
- Lime wedges, for serving
- Fresh cilantro, chopped (optional, for garnish)

Instructions:

1. Prepare the Pad Thai Sauce:
    - In a small bowl, whisk together tamarind paste, fish sauce, soy sauce, brown sugar, rice vinegar, chili flakes, and water until well combined. Set aside.
2. Cook the Rice Noodles:
    - Cook the rice noodles according to the package instructions until they are al dente. Drain and rinse with cold water to stop cooking. Set aside.
3. Cook the Tofu (or Protein of Choice):
    - Heat 1 tablespoon of vegetable oil in a large skillet or wok over medium-high heat.
    - Add the cubed tofu and cook until golden brown on all sides. Remove from the skillet and set aside.
4. Stir-Fry the Pad Thai:
    - In the same skillet, heat the remaining 1 tablespoon of vegetable oil over medium-high heat.
    - Add minced garlic and stir-fry for about 30 seconds until fragrant.

- Push the garlic to the side of the skillet and add the lightly beaten eggs. Scramble the eggs until they are cooked through.
5. Combine Everything:
    - Add the cooked rice noodles and prepared Pad Thai sauce to the skillet. Toss everything together gently to coat the noodles evenly with the sauce.
    - Add cooked tofu (or shrimp/chicken), bean sprouts, and sliced green onions to the skillet. Stir-fry for another 1-2 minutes until heated through.
6. Serve:
    - Remove from heat and transfer Pad Thai to serving plates.
    - Sprinkle chopped roasted peanuts on top and garnish with lime wedges and fresh cilantro (if using).
    - Serve hot and enjoy immediately.

Tips:

- Tamarind Paste: If you can't find tamarind paste, you can substitute with lime juice mixed with a bit of brown sugar.
- Protein Options: Feel free to customize Pad Thai with your choice of protein such as shrimp, chicken, or even beef.
- Adjust Seasoning: Taste the Pad Thai before serving and adjust the seasoning if needed with more fish sauce for saltiness, sugar for sweetness, or chili flakes for heat.

Pad Thai is a versatile dish that can be customized to your taste preferences. It's a crowd-pleaser and perfect for a weeknight dinner or when you're craving something deliciously Thai!

Italian Sausage Pasta

Ingredients:

- 1 lb Italian sausage links (sweet or spicy), casings removed
- 1 tablespoon olive oil
- 1 onion, diced
- 3 cloves garlic, minced
- 1 can (28 oz) crushed tomatoes
- 1 teaspoon dried oregano
- 1/2 teaspoon dried basil
- 1/4 teaspoon red pepper flakes (optional, for heat)
- Salt and freshly ground black pepper, to taste
- 1 lb pasta (such as penne, fusilli, or spaghetti)
- Fresh basil leaves, chopped, for garnish
- Grated Parmesan cheese, for serving

Instructions:

1. Cook the Italian Sausage:
    - In a large skillet or Dutch oven, heat olive oil over medium-high heat.
    - Add the Italian sausage (casings removed) to the skillet, breaking it up into small pieces with a spoon or spatula.
    - Cook the sausage until browned and cooked through, stirring occasionally. Remove the cooked sausage from the skillet and set aside.
2. Sauté the Onion and Garlic:
    - In the same skillet, add diced onion. Cook for about 3-4 minutes until onion becomes translucent and starts to soften.
    - Add minced garlic to the skillet and cook for another 1-2 minutes until fragrant.
3. Make the Tomato Sauce:
    - Pour crushed tomatoes into the skillet with the onion and garlic.
    - Add dried oregano, dried basil, red pepper flakes (if using), salt, and black pepper. Stir well to combine.
    - Bring the sauce to a simmer, then reduce the heat to low. Let it simmer gently for about 15-20 minutes to allow the flavors to meld together and the sauce to thicken slightly.
4. Cook the Pasta:
    - While the sauce is simmering, cook the pasta in a large pot of salted boiling water according to the package instructions until al dente.
    - Reserve about 1/2 cup of pasta cooking water before draining.
5. Combine Everything:
    - Add the cooked Italian sausage back into the skillet with the tomato sauce. Stir to combine and let it simmer for another few minutes.

- Add the drained pasta to the skillet and toss everything together gently. If the sauce seems too thick, add some of the reserved pasta cooking water to loosen it up.
6. Serve:
    - Serve the Italian Sausage Pasta hot, garnished with chopped fresh basil leaves and grated Parmesan cheese.
    - Enjoy immediately with crusty bread on the side, if desired.

Tips:

- Variations: Feel free to add extra vegetables such as bell peppers, mushrooms, or spinach to the sauce for added flavor and nutrition.
- Spice Level: Adjust the amount of red pepper flakes to your preference. You can omit them entirely if you prefer a milder dish.
- Make-Ahead: This pasta dish can be made ahead of time and stored in the refrigerator for a few days. Reheat gently on the stove with a splash of water or broth to freshen it up before serving.

This Italian Sausage Pasta is hearty, satisfying, and perfect for a comforting family dinner. It's sure to become a favorite!

Lemon Herb Roasted Vegetables

Ingredients:

- 1 lb mixed vegetables, such as:
    - Cherry tomatoes
    - Zucchini, sliced
    - Bell peppers, sliced
    - Red onion, sliced
    - Carrots, sliced
    - Brussels sprouts, halved
- 2 tablespoons olive oil
- Zest of 1 lemon
- Juice of 1 lemon
- 2 cloves garlic, minced
- 1 teaspoon dried thyme (or 1 tablespoon fresh thyme leaves)
- 1 teaspoon dried rosemary (or 1 tablespoon fresh rosemary, chopped)
- Salt and freshly ground black pepper, to taste
- Fresh parsley, chopped, for garnish (optional)

Instructions:

1. Preheat the Oven:
    - Preheat your oven to 425°F (220°C).
2. Prepare the Vegetables:
    - Wash and prepare the vegetables as needed. Cut larger vegetables into similar-sized pieces for even cooking.
3. Make the Lemon Herb Marinade:
    - In a small bowl, whisk together olive oil, lemon zest, lemon juice, minced garlic, dried thyme, dried rosemary, salt, and black pepper.
4. Coat the Vegetables:
    - Place the prepared vegetables in a large mixing bowl.
    - Pour the lemon herb marinade over the vegetables and toss well to coat evenly.
5. Roast the Vegetables:
    - Spread the vegetables in a single layer on a large baking sheet lined with parchment paper or aluminum foil.
    - Roast in the preheated oven for 25-30 minutes, or until the vegetables are tender and lightly browned, stirring halfway through cooking for even browning.
6. Serve:
    - Remove the roasted vegetables from the oven and transfer to a serving dish.
    - Garnish with chopped fresh parsley, if desired, and serve hot as a delicious side dish.

Tips:

- Variations: Feel free to customize the vegetables based on what you have on hand or your preferences. Other great additions include asparagus, eggplant, sweet potatoes, or cauliflower.
- Fresh Herbs: If using fresh herbs, add them towards the end of roasting to preserve their flavors.
- Leftovers: Store any leftover roasted vegetables in an airtight container in the refrigerator for up to 3-4 days. They can be reheated in the oven or microwave.

Enjoy these lemon herb roasted vegetables as a flavorful and nutritious addition to any meal, perfect for showcasing seasonal produce!

Hawaiian BBQ Chicken Pizza

Ingredients:

- 1 lb pizza dough (homemade or store-bought)
- 1/2 cup BBQ sauce (use your favorite variety)
- 1 cup cooked and shredded chicken breast
- 1 cup shredded mozzarella cheese
- 1/2 cup diced pineapple (fresh or canned)
- 1/4 cup diced red onion
- Fresh cilantro, chopped (for garnish, optional)
- Olive oil, for brushing

Instructions:

1. Preheat the Oven:
   - Preheat your oven to the temperature specified for your pizza dough (typically around 450°F/230°C).
2. Prepare the Pizza Dough:
   - On a lightly floured surface, roll out the pizza dough into your desired shape (round, rectangular, etc.). Transfer the dough to a pizza stone or baking sheet that has been lightly greased or lined with parchment paper.
3. Assemble the Pizza:
   - Brush the rolled-out pizza dough lightly with olive oil.
   - Spread the BBQ sauce evenly over the dough, leaving a small border around the edges for the crust.
   - Sprinkle the shredded mozzarella cheese over the BBQ sauce.
   - Scatter the shredded chicken, diced pineapple, and diced red onion evenly over the cheese.
4. Bake the Pizza:
   - Place the assembled pizza in the preheated oven and bake according to the pizza dough instructions, typically for 12-15 minutes or until the crust is golden brown and the cheese is melted and bubbly.
5. Garnish and Serve:
   - Remove the pizza from the oven and let it cool slightly.
   - Garnish with chopped fresh cilantro, if desired, for a burst of freshness and color.
   - Slice the pizza and serve hot.

Tips:

- Chicken: You can use leftover grilled or roasted chicken for this recipe, or quickly cook chicken breast by sautéing or boiling it and then shredding it.
- BBQ Sauce: Choose a BBQ sauce that you enjoy, whether it's sweet and tangy, smoky, or spicy, to complement the flavors of the pizza.

- Pineapple: If using canned pineapple, make sure to drain it well before using to prevent the pizza from becoming too watery.
- Customization: Feel free to add extra toppings such as crispy bacon, sliced jalapeños for a spicy kick, or bell peppers for more color and flavor.

This Hawaiian BBQ Chicken Pizza is perfect for a fun and flavorful dinner, combining the best of BBQ and tropical flavors in every bite. Enjoy making and indulging in this homemade pizza treat!

Pork Stir-fry with Snow Peas

Ingredients:

- 1 lb pork tenderloin or pork loin, thinly sliced
- 2 cups snow peas, ends trimmed
- 1 red bell pepper, sliced
- 1 onion, thinly sliced
- 3 cloves garlic, minced
- 1-inch piece of ginger, minced or grated
- 2 tablespoons soy sauce
- 1 tablespoon oyster sauce
- 1 tablespoon hoisin sauce
- 1 tablespoon rice vinegar
- 1 teaspoon sesame oil
- 1 tablespoon cornstarch
- 1/4 cup chicken broth or water
- 2 tablespoons vegetable oil, for stir-frying
- Cooked rice, for serving

Instructions:

1. Prepare the Pork:
    - In a bowl, combine the thinly sliced pork with soy sauce, oyster sauce, hoisin sauce, rice vinegar, sesame oil, and cornstarch. Mix well and let it marinate for about 15-20 minutes.
2. Stir-Fry the Vegetables:
    - Heat 1 tablespoon of vegetable oil in a large skillet or wok over medium-high heat.
    - Add minced garlic and ginger, and stir-fry for about 30 seconds until fragrant.
    - Add sliced onion and red bell pepper to the skillet. Stir-fry for 2-3 minutes until the vegetables start to soften.
3. Cook the Pork:
    - Push the vegetables to the side of the skillet and add the marinated pork slices in a single layer.
    - Cook the pork for about 2-3 minutes per side until browned and cooked through. Stir occasionally to ensure even cooking.
4. Add Snow Peas and Sauce:
    - Add snow peas to the skillet and stir-fry for another 1-2 minutes until they are bright green and crisp-tender.
5. Finish and Serve:
    - Pour chicken broth or water into the skillet to deglaze and create a sauce. Stir everything together gently until the sauce thickens slightly.
    - Taste and adjust seasoning if needed with more soy sauce or salt.

- Serve the pork stir-fry hot over cooked rice.

Tips:

- Vegetable Variation: Feel free to add other vegetables like sliced mushrooms, baby corn, or bamboo shoots to the stir-fry.
- Protein Substitution: Instead of pork, you can use thinly sliced chicken breast or beef steak strips.
- Spice it Up: Add a pinch of red pepper flakes or sliced fresh chili peppers for a spicy kick.

This pork stir-fry with snow peas is a versatile dish that's perfect for a quick weeknight meal. It's colorful, flavorful, and pairs wonderfully with steamed rice or noodles. Enjoy the delicious blend of tender pork and crisp vegetables in every bite!

Quinoa Stuffed Bell Peppers

Ingredients:

- 4 large bell peppers, any color
- 1 cup quinoa, rinsed
- 2 cups vegetable broth or water
- 1 tablespoon olive oil
- 1 onion, diced
- 2 cloves garlic, minced
- 1 zucchini, diced
- 1 carrot, diced
- 1 cup corn kernels (fresh, frozen, or canned)
- 1 can (15 oz) black beans, drained and rinsed
- 1 teaspoon ground cumin
- 1 teaspoon paprika
- Salt and freshly ground black pepper, to taste
- 1 cup shredded cheese (cheddar, mozzarella, or your favorite)
- Fresh cilantro or parsley, chopped, for garnish (optional)

Instructions:

1. **Prepare the Quinoa:**
    - In a medium saucepan, bring the vegetable broth or water to a boil.
    - Add quinoa, reduce heat to low, cover, and simmer for about 15 minutes or until quinoa is cooked and liquid is absorbed. Remove from heat and fluff with a fork.
2. **Prepare the Bell Peppers:**
    - Preheat your oven to 375°F (190°C).
    - Cut the tops off the bell peppers and remove the seeds and membranes from inside.
    - Place the bell peppers upright in a baking dish lined with parchment paper or lightly greased.
3. **Make the Filling:**
    - In a large skillet, heat olive oil over medium heat.
    - Add diced onion and garlic, and sauté until onion becomes translucent and garlic is fragrant, about 2-3 minutes.
    - Add diced zucchini, carrot, and corn kernels to the skillet. Cook for another 5-7 minutes until vegetables are tender.
4. **Combine the Filling:**
    - Stir in cooked quinoa, black beans, ground cumin, paprika, salt, and black pepper into the skillet with the sautéed vegetables. Mix well until evenly combined.
5. **Stuff the Bell Peppers:**
    - Spoon the quinoa and vegetable mixture evenly into each bell pepper until they are filled to the top.
    - Press the filling down gently with the back of a spoon.
6. **Bake the Stuffed Bell Peppers:**

- Cover the baking dish with foil and bake in the preheated oven for 25-30 minutes.
- Remove the foil and sprinkle shredded cheese on top of each stuffed bell pepper.
- Bake uncovered for an additional 5-7 minutes, or until the cheese is melted and bubbly.

7. Serve:
    - Remove the stuffed bell peppers from the oven and let them cool slightly.
    - Garnish with chopped fresh cilantro or parsley, if desired, before serving.

Tips:

- **Variations:** Feel free to customize the filling with other vegetables such as spinach, mushrooms, or diced tomatoes.
- **Protein Boost:** Add cooked ground meat (such as turkey, chicken, or beef) to the filling for extra protein.
- **Make-Ahead:** You can prepare the quinoa and filling mixture ahead of time and assemble the stuffed bell peppers just before baking.

These quinoa stuffed bell peppers are not only delicious but also a great way to incorporate nutritious ingredients into your meal. They make a satisfying vegetarian main dish or a flavorful side dish for any occasion!

Chicken Enchiladas

Ingredients:

For the Enchiladas:

- 1 lb boneless, skinless chicken breasts (about 2 large breasts)
- Salt and pepper, to taste
- 1 tablespoon olive oil
- 1 small onion, finely chopped
- 2 cloves garlic, minced
- 1 can (4 oz) diced green chilies, drained
- 1 teaspoon ground cumin
- 1 teaspoon chili powder
- 1/2 teaspoon paprika
- 1/4 teaspoon cayenne pepper (optional, for heat)
- 1/2 cup sour cream
- 1 cup shredded Monterey Jack or cheddar cheese
- 8-10 corn tortillas

For the Enchilada Sauce:

- 2 tablespoons olive oil
- 2 tablespoons all-purpose flour
- 1 tablespoon chili powder
- 1 teaspoon ground cumin
- 1/2 teaspoon garlic powder
- 1/4 teaspoon dried oregano
- 1/4 teaspoon salt
- 1/4 teaspoon freshly ground black pepper
- 2 cups chicken broth
- 1 can (8 oz) tomato sauce

Optional Garnishes:

- Chopped fresh cilantro
- Diced avocado
- Sliced jalapeños
- Sour cream
- Sliced green onions

Instructions:

1. Prepare the Chicken:
    - Season chicken breasts with salt and pepper on both sides.
    - In a large skillet, heat olive oil over medium-high heat.
    - Add chicken breasts and cook until browned on both sides and cooked through, about 5-7 minutes per side, depending on thickness.

- Remove chicken from skillet and shred using two forks or chop into small pieces. Set aside.
2. Make the Enchilada Sauce:
    - In the same skillet, add olive oil over medium heat.
    - Stir in flour and cook for 1 minute, stirring constantly.
    - Add chili powder, cumin, garlic powder, oregano, salt, and pepper. Cook for an additional 30 seconds to toast the spices.
    - Gradually whisk in chicken broth and tomato sauce. Bring to a simmer and cook for 5-10 minutes, stirring occasionally, until the sauce thickens slightly. Remove from heat.
3. Prepare the Filling:
    - In a separate skillet, heat a tablespoon of olive oil over medium heat.
    - Add chopped onion and cook until softened, about 3-4 minutes.
    - Add minced garlic, diced green chilies, ground cumin, chili powder, paprika, and cayenne pepper (if using). Cook for 1 minute until fragrant.
    - Stir in shredded chicken and sour cream. Cook for an additional 2-3 minutes until heated through. Remove from heat.
4. Assemble the Enchiladas:
    - Preheat your oven to 350°F (175°C).
    - Spread a thin layer of enchilada sauce on the bottom of a 9x13-inch baking dish.
    - Warm the corn tortillas briefly in the microwave or on a skillet until they are pliable.
    - Spoon about 1/4 cup of the chicken mixture onto each tortilla, roll up tightly, and place seam side down in the baking dish.
    - Continue until all tortillas are filled and rolled.
5. Bake the Enchiladas:
    - Pour the remaining enchilada sauce evenly over the rolled tortillas.
    - Sprinkle shredded cheese over the top of the enchiladas.
    - Cover the baking dish with aluminum foil and bake in the preheated oven for 20-25 minutes, until the cheese is melted and the enchiladas are heated through.
6. Serve:
    - Remove from the oven and let cool for a few minutes.
    - Garnish with chopped fresh cilantro, diced avocado, sliced jalapeños, sour cream, and sliced green onions, if desired.
    - Serve warm and enjoy!

Tips:

- Make-Ahead: You can prepare the enchiladas ahead of time and refrigerate them (covered) before baking. Just increase the baking time slightly if baking from cold.
- Variations: Feel free to customize the filling with additional ingredients such as black beans, diced tomatoes, or bell peppers.
- Tortillas: Corn tortillas are traditional for enchiladas, but you can use flour tortillas if preferred.

These chicken enchiladas are a crowd-pleasing favorite, perfect for family dinners or gatherings. They're comforting, flavorful, and sure to satisfy everyone at the table!

Creamy Mushroom Soup

Ingredients:

- 1 lb (450g) mushrooms, sliced (use a variety like button mushrooms, cremini, or shiitake)
- 2 tablespoons unsalted butter
- 1 onion, chopped
- 2 cloves garlic, minced
- 1 teaspoon fresh thyme leaves (or 1/2 teaspoon dried thyme)
- Salt and pepper, to taste
- 3 cups vegetable or chicken broth
- 1 cup heavy cream (or half-and-half for a lighter version)
- 2 tablespoons all-purpose flour (optional, for thickening)
- Fresh parsley, chopped, for garnish (optional)

Instructions:

1. Sauté the Mushrooms:
    - In a large pot or Dutch oven, melt the butter over medium heat.
    - Add chopped onion and sauté for 3-4 minutes until softened.
    - Add minced garlic and fresh thyme leaves, and sauté for another 1-2 minutes until fragrant.
2. Cook the Mushrooms:
    - Add sliced mushrooms to the pot. Cook, stirring occasionally, for about 8-10 minutes until the mushrooms release their moisture and brown slightly.
3. Make the Soup Base:
    - Season with salt and pepper to taste.
    - Pour in the vegetable or chicken broth and bring to a simmer. Let it simmer for about 15 minutes to allow the flavors to meld together.
4. Blend the Soup (Optional Step):
    - For a smooth and creamy texture, you can blend part or all of the soup. Use an immersion blender directly in the pot, or transfer a portion of the soup to a blender (in batches if necessary) and blend until smooth. Be cautious with hot liquids in blenders.
5. Add Cream and Thicken (Optional):
    - Stir in the heavy cream (or half-and-half) into the soup. Let it simmer gently for another 5 minutes.
    - If you prefer a thicker soup, mix 2 tablespoons of all-purpose flour with a little bit of cold water to form a slurry. Stir the slurry into the soup and simmer for a few more minutes until thickened.
6. Serve:
    - Ladle the creamy mushroom soup into bowls.
    - Garnish with chopped fresh parsley, if desired.
    - Serve hot with crusty bread or garlic toast on the side.

Tips:

- Variations: Add a splash of white wine or a dash of Worcestershire sauce for additional depth of flavor.
- Texture: If you prefer a chunkier soup, you can leave the mushrooms and onions in larger pieces without blending.
- Storage: Store leftover mushroom soup in an airtight container in the refrigerator for up to 3-4 days. Reheat gently on the stove, adding a splash of broth or cream to thin if needed.

This creamy mushroom soup is perfect for warming up on a chilly day or as a starter for a special meal. It's hearty, comforting, and sure to be a hit with mushroom lovers!

Shrimp Fried Rice

Ingredients:

- 1 lb (450g) medium shrimp, peeled and deveined
- 3 cups cooked rice (preferably day-old and cooled)
- 2 tablespoons soy sauce
- 1 tablespoon oyster sauce
- 1 teaspoon sesame oil
- 2 tablespoons vegetable oil, divided
- 2 cloves garlic, minced
- 1 onion, diced
- 1 carrot, diced
- 1 cup frozen peas, thawed
- 2 eggs, lightly beaten
- Salt and pepper, to taste
- Green onions, chopped (for garnish)
- Sesame seeds (for garnish, optional)

Instructions:

1. Prepare the Shrimp:
   - Season the shrimp with salt and pepper.
   - In a large skillet or wok, heat 1 tablespoon of vegetable oil over medium-high heat.
   - Add the shrimp and cook for 2-3 minutes per side until pink and cooked through. Remove from the skillet and set aside.
2. Cook the Vegetables:
   - In the same skillet, heat the remaining tablespoon of vegetable oil over medium heat.
   - Add minced garlic and diced onion. Cook for 2-3 minutes until onion becomes translucent.
   - Add diced carrot and cook for another 2-3 minutes until carrot starts to soften.
   - Stir in thawed peas and cook for 1 minute. Remove the vegetables from the skillet and set aside.
3. Scramble the Eggs:
   - Push the vegetables to the side of the skillet and pour the lightly beaten eggs into the empty space.
   - Let the eggs cook for a few seconds until they start to set, then scramble them with a spatula until cooked through.
   - Mix the scrambled eggs with the cooked vegetables in the skillet.
4. Combine Everything:
   - Add the cooked rice to the skillet with the vegetables and eggs.
   - Pour soy sauce, oyster sauce, and sesame oil over the rice mixture. Stir well to combine and coat everything evenly.

- Cook for 2-3 minutes, stirring frequently, until the rice is heated through and starts to lightly crisp.
5. **Add Shrimp and Finish:**
    - Gently fold in the cooked shrimp until evenly distributed throughout the fried rice.
    - Taste and adjust seasoning with additional soy sauce, salt, or pepper if needed.
6. **Serve:**
    - Transfer the shrimp fried rice to serving plates or bowls.
    - Garnish with chopped green onions and sesame seeds, if desired.
    - Serve hot and enjoy your homemade shrimp fried rice!

Tips:

- Rice: Day-old rice works best for fried rice as it is drier and holds up better during cooking. If using freshly cooked rice, spread it out on a baking sheet to cool quickly before using.
- Vegetables: Feel free to customize the vegetables based on your preferences. You can add bell peppers, mushrooms, or broccoli florets.
- Storage: Store any leftovers in an airtight container in the refrigerator for up to 3 days. Reheat gently in the microwave or skillet with a splash of water or broth to freshen it up.

This shrimp fried rice recipe is versatile and perfect for a quick weeknight dinner. It's packed with flavor and makes a satisfying meal on its own or as a side dish with other Asian-inspired dishes. Enjoy cooking and indulging in this homemade favorite!

Greek Lemon Chicken Skewers

Ingredients:

- 1.5 lbs (about 700g) boneless, skinless chicken breasts or thighs, cut into 1-inch cubes
- Zest and juice of 1-2 lemons (about 1/4 cup lemon juice)
- 3 cloves garlic, minced
- 2 tablespoons olive oil
- 1 tablespoon dried oregano
- 1 teaspoon dried thyme
- 1 teaspoon dried rosemary
- 1/2 teaspoon paprika
- Salt and freshly ground black pepper, to taste
- Wooden or metal skewers (if using wooden skewers, soak them in water for 30 minutes before using)

Instructions:

1. Prepare the Marinade:
    - In a large bowl, combine lemon zest, lemon juice, minced garlic, olive oil, dried oregano, dried thyme, dried rosemary, paprika, salt, and black pepper. Mix well to combine.
2. Marinate the Chicken:
    - Add the chicken cubes to the marinade and toss to coat thoroughly. Cover the bowl with plastic wrap or transfer to a sealed container.
    - Marinate in the refrigerator for at least 1 hour, or ideally overnight, to allow the flavors to meld together.
3. Skewer the Chicken:
    - Preheat your grill or grill pan over medium-high heat.
    - Thread the marinated chicken cubes onto skewers, distributing them evenly and leaving a little space between each piece.
4. Grill the Skewers:
    - Brush the grill grates lightly with oil to prevent sticking.
    - Place the chicken skewers on the preheated grill and cook for 5-7 minutes per side, or until the chicken is cooked through and has nice grill marks. Turn occasionally to cook all sides evenly.
5. Serve:
    - Remove the cooked chicken skewers from the grill and let them rest for a few minutes.
    - Serve hot, garnished with fresh herbs like parsley or dill, if desired.
    - Enjoy your Greek lemon chicken skewers with sides like tzatziki sauce, Greek salad, or rice pilaf.

Tips:

- Variations: Feel free to add vegetables like bell peppers, onions, or cherry tomatoes between the chicken pieces on the skewers for added flavor and color.
- Oven-Baked Option: If you prefer, you can bake the skewers in the oven at 400°F (200°C) for about 20-25 minutes, or until the chicken is fully cooked through.
- Serve with: Greek lemon chicken skewers are delicious on their own or served with pita bread, couscous, or roasted vegetables.

These Greek lemon chicken skewers are perfect for a summer barbecue or a weeknight dinner. They're easy to make and packed with Mediterranean flavors that everyone will love!

Sweet and Sour Meatballs

Ingredients:

For the Meatballs:

- 1 lb ground beef or pork (or a combination)
- 1/2 cup breadcrumbs
- 1/4 cup milk
- 1 egg
- 1/2 teaspoon salt
- 1/4 teaspoon black pepper
- 1/2 teaspoon garlic powder
- 1/2 teaspoon onion powder
- 1 tablespoon vegetable oil (for cooking meatballs)

For the Sweet and Sour Sauce:

- 1/2 cup ketchup
- 1/4 cup rice vinegar
- 1/4 cup brown sugar
- 1 tablespoon soy sauce
- 1 teaspoon Worcestershire sauce
- 1/2 cup water or pineapple juice (for a fruity twist)
- 1 tablespoon cornstarch
- 1/4 cup water (for cornstarch slurry)

Optional Additions:

- 1 bell pepper, diced
- 1 onion, diced
- Pineapple chunks (canned or fresh)

Instructions:

1. Make the Meatballs:
   - In a large bowl, combine ground meat, breadcrumbs, milk, egg, salt, pepper, garlic powder, and onion powder. Mix until well combined.
   - Shape the mixture into meatballs, about 1 inch in diameter.
2. Cook the Meatballs:
   - Heat vegetable oil in a large skillet over medium-high heat.
   - Add the meatballs to the skillet in a single layer (you may need to work in batches).
   - Cook the meatballs, turning occasionally, until browned on all sides and cooked through, about 10-12 minutes. Remove from the skillet and set aside.

3. Make the Sweet and Sour Sauce:
    - In the same skillet (remove excess oil if necessary), combine ketchup, rice vinegar, brown sugar, soy sauce, Worcestershire sauce, and water or pineapple juice.
    - Bring the sauce to a simmer over medium heat, stirring occasionally.
4. Thicken the Sauce:
    - In a small bowl, mix cornstarch with water to create a slurry.
    - Gradually add the cornstarch slurry to the simmering sauce, stirring constantly.
    - Continue to simmer for 2-3 minutes, or until the sauce has thickened to your desired consistency.
5. Combine Meatballs and Sauce:
    - Return the cooked meatballs to the skillet with the sweet and sour sauce.
    - Add diced bell pepper, onion, and pineapple chunks (if using).
    - Stir gently to coat the meatballs and vegetables evenly with the sauce.
6. Simmer and Serve:
    - Simmer the meatballs in the sauce for an additional 5-7 minutes, stirring occasionally, until heated through and the flavors have melded together.
    - Serve hot over steamed rice or noodles, garnished with chopped green onions or sesame seeds, if desired.

Tips:

- Make-Ahead: You can prepare the meatballs ahead of time and store them in the refrigerator until ready to cook.
- Variations: Feel free to customize the sauce by adjusting the sweetness or tanginess to your taste. You can also add other vegetables like carrots or snap peas.
- Gluten-Free Option: Use gluten-free breadcrumbs or oats, and ensure your soy sauce and Worcestershire sauce are gluten-free.

These sweet and sour meatballs are perfect for a hearty dinner or as a crowd-pleasing appetizer for parties. They're flavorful, comforting, and sure to be a hit with family and friends!

Caprese Pasta Salad

Ingredients:

- 8 oz (225g) pasta (such as fusilli, penne, or farfalle)
- 1 pint cherry tomatoes, halved
- 8 oz (225g) fresh mozzarella pearls (or mozzarella cut into small cubes)
- 1/2 cup fresh basil leaves, chopped or torn
- 1/4 cup extra virgin olive oil
- 2 tablespoons balsamic vinegar
- 2 cloves garlic, minced (optional)
- Salt and freshly ground black pepper, to taste
- Fresh basil leaves, for garnish (optional)

Instructions:

1. Cook the Pasta:
    - Bring a large pot of salted water to a boil.
    - Cook the pasta according to package instructions until al dente. Drain and rinse under cold water to stop the cooking process. Let it cool completely.
2. Prepare the Dressing:
    - In a small bowl, whisk together extra virgin olive oil, balsamic vinegar, minced garlic (if using), salt, and black pepper.
3. Assemble the Salad:
    - In a large salad bowl, combine the cooked and cooled pasta, halved cherry tomatoes, mozzarella pearls (or cubed mozzarella), and chopped basil.
    - Pour the dressing over the salad ingredients and toss gently to combine, ensuring everything is coated evenly.
4. Chill and Serve:
    - Cover the salad bowl with plastic wrap or transfer to an airtight container.
    - Refrigerate for at least 30 minutes to allow the flavors to meld together.
5. Garnish and Serve:
    - Before serving, garnish with additional fresh basil leaves if desired.
    - Serve chilled as a refreshing side dish or light meal.

Tips:

- Variations: You can add extras like grilled chicken, avocado slices, or pine nuts for added flavor and texture.
- Make-Ahead: This salad can be made ahead of time and stored in the refrigerator for up to 2 days. Add fresh basil just before serving for the best flavor.
- Gluten-Free Option: Use gluten-free pasta to make this dish gluten-free.

This Caprese pasta salad is perfect for picnics, potlucks, or as a light summer meal. It's fresh, vibrant, and showcases the classic Caprese flavors beautifully!

Butternut Squash Risotto

Ingredients:

- 1 small butternut squash (about 2 lbs), peeled, seeded, and cut into 1/2-inch cubes
- 6 cups vegetable or chicken broth (low-sodium)
- 2 tablespoons olive oil
- 1 onion, finely chopped
- 2 cloves garlic, minced
- 1 1/2 cups Arborio rice
- 1/2 cup dry white wine (optional)
- 1/2 teaspoon dried thyme (or 1 teaspoon fresh thyme leaves)
- Salt and freshly ground black pepper, to taste
- 1/2 cup grated Parmesan cheese
- 2 tablespoons unsalted butter
- Fresh parsley, chopped (for garnish, optional)

Instructions:

1. Prepare the Butternut Squash:
   - Preheat your oven to 400°F (200°C).
   - Place the butternut squash cubes on a baking sheet. Drizzle with 1 tablespoon of olive oil and season with salt and pepper. Toss to coat evenly.
   - Roast the butternut squash in the preheated oven for 20-25 minutes, or until tender and lightly caramelized. Set aside.
2. Prepare the Broth:
   - In a saucepan, heat the vegetable or chicken broth over medium heat until simmering. Reduce the heat to low and keep the broth warm.
3. Cook the Risotto:
   - In a large skillet or Dutch oven, heat the remaining tablespoon of olive oil over medium heat.
   - Add chopped onion and sauté for 3-4 minutes until softened.
   - Add minced garlic and cook for another 1 minute until fragrant.
4. Toast the Rice:
   - Add Arborio rice to the skillet with the onion and garlic. Cook, stirring constantly, for 1-2 minutes until the rice grains are lightly toasted.
5. Deglaze with Wine (Optional):
   - Pour in the white wine (if using) and stir until the liquid is absorbed by the rice.
6. Add the Broth:
   - Begin adding the warm broth to the rice mixture, one ladleful at a time, stirring frequently.
   - Allow each addition of broth to be absorbed before adding the next ladleful. This process will take about 20-25 minutes. The rice should be creamy and tender, with a slight bite (al dente).

7. Incorporate Butternut Squash:
    - Stir in the roasted butternut squash cubes during the last 5 minutes of cooking. This allows the squash to heat through and blend with the risotto.
8. Finish the Risotto:
    - Once the rice is cooked to your desired consistency, remove the skillet from the heat.
    - Stir in grated Parmesan cheese and butter until melted and creamy.
    - Season with salt, pepper, and dried thyme (or fresh thyme leaves), adjusting to taste.
9. Serve:
    - Spoon the butternut squash risotto into serving bowls.
    - Garnish with chopped fresh parsley, if desired.
    - Serve hot and enjoy the creamy, comforting flavors of butternut squash risotto!

Tips:

- Variations: Add cooked bacon or pancetta for a savory twist, or stir in baby spinach or kale for added greens.
- Storage: Leftover risotto can be stored in an airtight container in the refrigerator for up to 3 days. Reheat gently on the stove with a splash of broth or water to loosen the consistency.

This butternut squash risotto recipe is perfect for a cozy dinner at home, showcasing the sweet and nutty flavors of roasted squash combined with creamy risotto rice. Enjoy this comforting dish with a glass of white wine for a delightful meal!

BBQ Chicken Quesadillas

Ingredients:

- 2 cups cooked and shredded chicken (rotisserie chicken works well)
- 1/2 cup barbecue sauce (use your favorite variety)
- 4 large flour tortillas
- 2 cups shredded cheese (cheddar, Monterey Jack, or a blend)
- 1/4 cup chopped red onion (optional)
- 2 tablespoons chopped fresh cilantro (optional)
- Cooking spray or olive oil

Instructions:

1. Prepare the BBQ Chicken:
    - In a bowl, mix the shredded chicken with barbecue sauce until well coated. Adjust the amount of sauce to your preference.
2. Assemble the Quesadillas:
    - Lay out the tortillas on a clean surface.
    - Divide the shredded cheese evenly among the tortillas, sprinkling it over half of each tortilla.
    - Spoon the BBQ chicken mixture over the cheese on each tortilla.
    - If using, sprinkle chopped red onion and fresh cilantro over the chicken.
3. Fold and Cook the Quesadillas:
    - Fold the tortillas in half over the filling to create a half-moon shape.
    - Heat a large skillet or griddle over medium heat. Lightly spray the skillet with cooking spray or brush with olive oil.
    - Carefully place one or two quesadillas (depending on the size of your skillet) into the hot skillet.
    - Cook for about 2-3 minutes on each side, or until the tortilla is golden brown and crispy, and the cheese is melted. Use a spatula to press down gently while cooking to help seal the quesadilla.
4. Serve:
    - Remove the quesadillas from the skillet and let them cool for a minute.
    - Cut each quesadilla into wedges using a sharp knife or pizza cutter.
    - Serve hot with sour cream, guacamole, salsa, or additional barbecue sauce for dipping.

Tips:

- Variations: Add sliced jalapeños, diced bell peppers, or cooked corn kernels to the filling for extra flavor and texture.

- Grilling Option: You can also grill the quesadillas on an outdoor grill. Just brush both sides lightly with olive oil and grill over medium heat until crispy and the cheese is melted.
- Make-Ahead: Prepare the BBQ chicken filling ahead of time and store it in the refrigerator until ready to assemble and cook the quesadillas.

These BBQ chicken quesadillas are perfect for a quick weeknight dinner or as a crowd-pleasing appetizer for parties. They're easy to customize and always a hit with both kids and adults alike!

Garlic Parmesan Roasted Shrimp

Ingredients:

- 1 lb (450g) large shrimp, peeled and deveined
- 3 cloves garlic, minced
- 2 tablespoons olive oil
- 1/4 cup grated Parmesan cheese
- 1 tablespoon fresh parsley, chopped (or 1 teaspoon dried parsley)
- 1/2 teaspoon paprika
- Salt and pepper, to taste
- Lemon wedges, for serving (optional)

Instructions:

1. Preheat the Oven:
   - Preheat your oven to 400°F (200°C). Line a baking sheet with parchment paper or foil for easy cleanup.
2. Prepare the Shrimp:
   - In a large bowl, combine the peeled and deveined shrimp with minced garlic, olive oil, grated Parmesan cheese, chopped parsley, paprika, salt, and pepper. Toss until the shrimp are evenly coated with the mixture.
3. Roast the Shrimp:
   - Spread the seasoned shrimp in a single layer on the prepared baking sheet.
   - Roast in the preheated oven for 8-10 minutes, or until the shrimp are pink and opaque, and the Parmesan cheese is melted and lightly golden.
4. Serve:
   - Remove the roasted shrimp from the oven.
   - Squeeze fresh lemon juice over the shrimp, if desired, for a bright finish.
   - Serve immediately as an appetizer with cocktail sauce or as a main dish over pasta or rice.

Tips:

- Variations: Add a pinch of red pepper flakes for a hint of spice, or garnish with additional chopped fresh herbs like basil or thyme.
- Side Suggestions: Garlic Parmesan roasted shrimp pairs well with a side of steamed vegetables, crusty bread, or a light salad.
- Storage: Store any leftover roasted shrimp in an airtight container in the refrigerator for up to 2 days. Reheat gently in the oven or microwave before serving.

This garlic Parmesan roasted shrimp recipe is quick and easy to prepare, making it perfect for both weeknight dinners and special occasions. Enjoy the robust flavors and tender texture of this delicious dish!

Turkey Meatloaf

Ingredients:

- 1 lb ground turkey (preferably lean)
- 1/2 cup breadcrumbs (plain or seasoned)
- 1/2 cup milk (or chicken broth)
- 1/2 cup grated Parmesan cheese
- 1 small onion, finely chopped
- 1 carrot, grated (optional, for added moisture and flavor)
- 1/2 cup chopped fresh parsley (or 2 tablespoons dried parsley)
- 2 cloves garlic, minced
- 1 egg, beaten
- 1 tablespoon Worcestershire sauce
- 1 teaspoon dried thyme
- 1 teaspoon dried oregano
- 1 teaspoon salt
- 1/2 teaspoon black pepper
- Olive oil or cooking spray

Glaze (optional):

- 1/4 cup ketchup
- 1 tablespoon brown sugar
- 1 tablespoon Dijon mustard

Instructions:

1. Preheat the Oven:
   - Preheat your oven to 375°F (190°C). Lightly grease a loaf pan with olive oil or cooking spray.
2. Prepare the Meatloaf Mixture:
   - In a large bowl, combine ground turkey, breadcrumbs, milk (or chicken broth), grated Parmesan cheese, finely chopped onion, grated carrot (if using), chopped parsley, minced garlic, beaten egg, Worcestershire sauce, dried thyme, dried oregano, salt, and black pepper.
   - Mix the ingredients together gently but thoroughly. Avoid overmixing to keep the meatloaf tender.
3. Shape the Meatloaf:
   - Transfer the meatloaf mixture into the prepared loaf pan. Use your hands to shape it into a loaf shape, pressing gently to compact the mixture.
4. Optional Glaze:
   - In a small bowl, mix together ketchup, brown sugar, and Dijon mustard to create the glaze.

- Spread the glaze evenly over the top of the meatloaf.
5. Bake the Meatloaf:
   - Place the meatloaf in the preheated oven and bake for 45-55 minutes, or until the internal temperature reaches 165°F (75°C) on an instant-read thermometer.
   - If using the glaze, it should be caramelized and slightly bubbly.
6. Rest and Serve:
   - Remove the turkey meatloaf from the oven and let it rest in the loaf pan for 5-10 minutes before slicing.
   - Slice and serve hot, garnished with additional chopped parsley if desired.

Tips:

- Vegetables: Feel free to add other finely chopped vegetables like bell peppers or celery for added flavor and texture.
- Leftovers: Turkey meatloaf leftovers can be stored in an airtight container in the refrigerator for up to 3 days. Reheat slices gently in the microwave or oven.

This turkey meatloaf recipe is a comforting and wholesome meal that's perfect for family dinners. It pairs well with mashed potatoes, steamed vegetables, or a fresh green salad. Enjoy the delicious flavors and the healthier twist with ground turkey!

Veggie Stir-fry with Tofu

Ingredients:

- 14 oz (400g) firm tofu, drained and cut into cubes
- 2 tablespoons soy sauce (or tamari for gluten-free)
- 1 tablespoon cornstarch
- 2 tablespoons vegetable oil, divided
- 1 onion, thinly sliced
- 2 bell peppers (any color), thinly sliced
- 1 cup broccoli florets
- 1 carrot, thinly sliced
- 1 cup snap peas or snow peas
- 3 cloves garlic, minced
- 1-inch piece of ginger, minced
- Optional: sliced mushrooms, baby corn, water chestnuts, or any other vegetables of your choice

Stir-fry Sauce:

- 1/4 cup soy sauce (or tamari)
- 2 tablespoons hoisin sauce
- 1 tablespoon rice vinegar
- 1 tablespoon sesame oil
- 1 tablespoon brown sugar or honey
- 1 teaspoon cornstarch
- 1/4 cup water

Instructions:

1. Prepare the Tofu:
    - In a bowl, toss the tofu cubes with 2 tablespoons of soy sauce and 1 tablespoon of cornstarch until evenly coated.
2. Cook the Tofu:
    - Heat 1 tablespoon of vegetable oil in a large skillet or wok over medium-high heat.
    - Add the tofu cubes in a single layer and cook until golden and crispy on all sides, about 4-5 minutes. Remove from the skillet and set aside.
3. Prepare the Stir-fry Sauce:
    - In a small bowl, whisk together 1/4 cup soy sauce (or tamari), hoisin sauce, rice vinegar, sesame oil, brown sugar (or honey), 1 teaspoon cornstarch, and 1/4 cup water until smooth. Set aside.
4. Stir-fry the Vegetables:

- In the same skillet or wok, heat the remaining 1 tablespoon of vegetable oil over medium-high heat.
- Add the sliced onion and stir-fry for 2 minutes until softened.
- Add the bell peppers, broccoli florets, sliced carrot, snap peas (or snow peas), and any other vegetables you're using. Stir-fry for 4-5 minutes until the vegetables are crisp-tender.

5. Add Garlic and Ginger:
    - Clear a small space in the center of the skillet and add the minced garlic and ginger. Cook for 1 minute until fragrant, then mix with the vegetables.
6. Combine Tofu and Sauce:
    - Return the cooked tofu cubes to the skillet with the vegetables.
    - Pour the prepared stir-fry sauce over everything in the skillet.
7. Simmer and Serve:
    - Stir everything together gently until the sauce thickens and coats the vegetables and tofu, about 1-2 minutes.
    - Taste and adjust seasoning if needed, adding more soy sauce or brown sugar as desired.
8. Serve:
    - Serve the veggie stir-fry with tofu hot over steamed rice or noodles.
    - Garnish with sliced green onions, sesame seeds, or chopped fresh cilantro, if desired.

Tips:

- Preparation: Have all your ingredients chopped and ready before you start cooking, as stir-frying happens quickly.
- Variations: Feel free to customize with your favorite vegetables like bok choy, cabbage, or zucchini.
- Protein: If you prefer, you can substitute tofu with tempeh or add cooked chicken, shrimp, or beef strips.

This veggie stir-fry with tofu is a nutritious and satisfying dish that's perfect for a quick weeknight dinner. It's packed with flavors and textures, making it a favorite for vegetarians and meat-eaters alike!

Lemon Garlic Butter Salmon

Ingredients:

- 4 salmon fillets, skin-on or skinless (about 6 oz each)
- Salt and pepper, to taste
- 2 tablespoons olive oil
- 4 tablespoons unsalted butter
- 4 cloves garlic, minced
- Zest and juice of 1 lemon
- 2 tablespoons chopped fresh parsley (optional, for garnish)

Instructions:

1. Prepare the Salmon:
   - Pat the salmon fillets dry with paper towels. Season both sides with salt and pepper to taste.
2. Cook the Salmon:
   - In a large skillet, heat the olive oil over medium-high heat until shimmering.
   - Place the salmon fillets in the skillet, skin-side down if they have skin. Cook for 4-5 minutes, without moving them, until golden and crispy.
   - Carefully flip the salmon fillets using a spatula and cook for an additional 3-4 minutes, or until the salmon is cooked to your desired doneness (145°F internal temperature for medium).
3. Make the Lemon Garlic Butter Sauce:
   - Reduce the heat to medium-low. Add the butter to the skillet and let it melt.
   - Add the minced garlic to the skillet and cook for 1-2 minutes, stirring constantly, until fragrant and lightly golden.
   - Stir in the lemon zest and lemon juice. Cook for another minute, allowing the flavors to meld together. Taste and adjust seasoning if needed.
4. Serve:
   - Remove the skillet from heat. Spoon the lemon garlic butter sauce over the salmon fillets.
   - Garnish with chopped fresh parsley, if desired.
5. Optional Serving Suggestion:
   - Serve the lemon garlic butter salmon with steamed vegetables, rice, or a fresh salad for a complete meal.

Tips:

- Variations: You can add capers, diced tomatoes, or spinach to the lemon garlic butter sauce for additional flavors.
- Skinless Salmon: If using skinless salmon fillets, cook each side for about 3-4 minutes depending on thickness.

- Broiling Option: You can also finish cooking the salmon under the broiler for a couple of minutes after searing for a crispier texture on top.

This lemon garlic butter salmon recipe is perfect for a quick and impressive dinner, whether you're cooking for yourself or entertaining guests. Enjoy the rich flavors of buttery salmon with a hint of citrus and garlic!